BALANCED
Living

by
Kay Spears

Dr. Bill,

Many blessings

Kay S____

Harrison House
Tulsa, Oklahoma

Balanced Living
Copyright © 2011 by Kay Spears.
ISBN: 978-160683-409-1

Published by :
Harrison House Publishers
Tulsa, OK 74145

Printed in the United States of America

$\mathcal{B}$alance is required in order to excel in this life.

Acknowledgements

I want to thank all of my dedicated clients who have been with me through the years. These people have become good friends of mine and they have always kept me going when I did not think I could continue. During the time of writing this book, I was trying to build my practice and finish my master's degree.

I want to thank my family and friends who believe in me sometimes more than I believe in myself.

I want to thank chiropractor Kevin Amen (mentioned in this book) for telling me that God loves me and explaining to me that I was not being punished. At that point in my life, I was so fragile and could have easily allowed my circumstances to take my life if it were not for Kevin's kind words of comfort and peace.

I want to thank Sandy Ross, my mentor, who has shown me all the wonderful scriptures that pertain to God's love for us all. Sandy guided me in my spiritual journey with God and showed me how God's promises of love and protection can always be trusted.

I want to thank my good friend Scott Avery, my biggest cheerleader. Scott helped me start this book. I never thought I could write a book, but Scott always makes me reach further to obtain my goals.

I would also like to thank the Feeleys who own River Rim Resort, a beautiful resort on the Frio River. The Feeleys provided me with a place to stay while I wrote most of this book. I am thankful for peace and balance that I could only feel in such a magical place. There is nothing like the hill country in Texas to show that God does exist.

I want to thank my dogs that inspire me every day to try to live a stress-free life and to love everyone around me.

Lastly, I want to recognize the most important relationship in my life, and that is my relationship with God. Thank you, God, for Your love, acceptance, and promises that are never empty, and thank You for never leaving my side.

Contents

Introduction

My hope is that this book will reach out to the many people who are looking for answers in this chaotic world. Life is so much more demanding than it used to be. We face more chronic degenerative diseases than ever before because we do not eat right and because we are missing important nutrients in our diet. We should be including supplements in our diet that help replace those missing nutrients.

We do not sleep enough, exercise enough, or drink enough water as the ever increasing hurry-up lifestyle takes over and we find that we do not have time to take care of ourselves. We have become so far from balanced that being "in balance" is starting to sound like a novel idea! And the results are showing up in our bodies.

This book is not just another nutrition book. I write about the steps to a balanced life, which include nutrition, supplementation, sleep, exercise, water, forgiveness, and an attitude of gratitude. I also write about my personal journey to inner peace and resolution in my own life. I believe that by sharing my experiences, I can save you time, money, and emotional stress in your own life. If you implement the steps in this book, you will stay balanced and will be able to stay healthy.

Two steps I include in this book to complete the seven steps are the importance of forgiveness and an attitude of gratitude. We typically do not forgive people, let alone forgive ourselves for wrongdoings. And too often, we are not thankful for what we have. I share in my book how my journey brought me to God and how God brought peace and love to my life in such an amazing way that I have to share it with you.

I am a Certified Clinical Nutritionist in San Antonio, Texas. I have my master's degree in nutrition and I have a thriving practice in the San Antonio area. I have been a nutritionist for over thirteen years. Nutrition is one of the steps in my book, it's what I know best, but as you will read, even though I knew all about nutrition, that alone was not enough to help me.

Before we jump into the core steps of balance, I want to invite you into my personal story. It takes a lot to put yourself and your story out there, but I wanted to share this with you so you could see the struggles I had to go through in order to achieve balance.

I really hope that this book will touch you for your quality of life is so very important. Enjoy life, because you only get one!

Balance

MY JOURNEY-MY STORY

Balance has so many dimensions to it. It is multifaceted, just like a diamond. What I thought was balance when I was younger … well, let's just say it's not how I would define balance today!

I have battled to find the balance between the extremes of overconfidence and fear, sickness and health, being a people-pleaser and rebelling, independence and dependence, risk and security, control and lack of it, sobriety and addiction, and more. These battles are themes that unite us all. I wanted to be unique, to be special, but many times I ended up simply being a statistic. That is not the life I wanted, and I know that is not the life that you want!

I've learned a lot along the way, and part of that has been the maturity and humility to accept help from others. Please know that my heart is to help you find balance.

For me, the struggle began in childhood. I have always been fending for myself. I felt abandoned by my parents when they got divorced. My mom left to start a new life in

California, and that life did not include me. My dad assumed full responsibility for raising his three kids, and while I appreciate his willingness to accept that challenge, it was too much for a man to do alone. He was busy trying to build a career at the same time, and he did the best he could, but there were holes in the parenting I received.

I was forced to be self-sufficient. I knew that nobody was going to pave my way. In fact, as a child, I was so independent that I had problems in school. I didn't need authority, I reasoned, so I rejected it.

I grew up being good at controlling everything around me. I was a go-getter, and I liked to do things my way. In my late teens and early 20s, I was just plain rebellious. I had been going out with a guy and I knew my family did not like him. I thought to myself, *I'll show them!*

What a silly thing to say, much less believe, and even less act upon! But we don't do the smartest things when we are so off kilter, do we?

So we got married. I was all of 20 years old, but I thought I was big enough to handle whatever life threw at me. But my I'll-show-you marriage hurt me more than anyone else. I spent five years in turmoil, drugs, and purely everything I did not want or need in my life.

I experienced physical and mental abuse and chronic nights of rocking in my closet because I needed more drugs. One morning, I looked at myself in the mirror and did not even recognize what I had become.

What had I done? Who was I? Did I deserve more?

Inside of me, I wanted more, but what could I do? As a young girl, I had struggled with weight issues and I decided that I wanted to go back to college to finish the dream of being healthy. I was by no means healthy, but that day in the bathroom, I decided what I wanted to do.

I walked away from my abusive husband and moved back home with my family in Texas. I enrolled in college to become a nutritionist.

Once again I was in charge, I was back on track ... or so I thought. I was working full-time and going to school, and all of a sudden I was knocked off track again by another guy.

Now, is it just me or do guys have a way of knocking us girls off track? Actually, I admit, I was barely on track. The slightest nudge would have been enough to derail me. And what's more, it was me who derailed myself.

Anyway, I always seemed to be drawn to guys who would tell me everything I needed to hear to feed my starving soul. I say this because I was starving for attention. My mother had told me that she wished she never had me and my father had told me that I was going to be barefoot and pregnant living in a trailer if I wasn't careful.

Do you have negative voices speaking into your life? If you do, you must first recognize that those words are lies, then find a way to feed yourself the truth.

Naturally, it seemed, I needed someone to tell me how special I was. The problem was that once my true colors became apparent and reality kicked in, that person would usually tell me how worthless I was. I would actually feel okay with those deriding words. In fact, those hurtful words felt even truer than the praise I wanted! That's what was so sad, but the hunger within me showed how out of balance I really was.

So when I fell for this guy, only to be mistreated again, I thought my world had come to an end. I ran! I went to California to lick my wounds and hopefully finish my degree.

According to my father, this was a "big waste of time," but since I still lived a life of rebellion, I didn't care what he said. It was another season of trying to escape from situations and to control my life, but the one bright spot was that I did eventually get my bachelor's degree in nutrition.

At that time, in my early 30s and with my degree under my belt, I decided to take a much-deserved break. I headed to Europe for eight weeks, and in typical fashion, I went on this trip by myself. I thought could take it on alone. After all, I was in control of my world.

This trip turned out to be the first time that I realized there was a force much bigger than me. I always believed in God (even though I did not really know what that meant), and God protected me from some things that could have cost me more pain than was already in my pain bank. I felt a presence with me the whole way. I traveled to France, Italy, Switzerland, Germany, Amsterdam, and Belgium. Feeling empowered and on top of the world, I traveled back home and quickly forgot about that unbelievable presence that was carrying me through Europe.

I came home to another urge from within. I wanted to go to graduate school and get my master's degree. This venture took some time and after months of studying and writing letters to get into the college I wanted to attend, I once again prevailed and was on my way.

After just one year in grad school, I met soon-to-be husband number two. He was eight years younger than me and full of life. Our time together was full of outdoor activities, which I loved. The relationship continued, but after four years of "hanging out" together, I decided it was time to start pressuring this guy to marry me.

Come on, my biological clock was ticking! He was going to marry me or we were going to move on. Have you ever been there? If you are there now, how much of the ticking noise is in your body and how much of the noise is in your head?

I pressed the issue, and he proposed. So, after winning that challenge, we set about planning our wedding. The problem was ... I could see trouble ahead. I knew it. I saw it. But I just chose to ignore it.

Now, I know you've never done that! If you haven't, trust me, it's not worth it. If you see trouble ahead, get off the road. Do a U-turn. Go back and reconsider the road you are on.

But I was obstinate and rebellious, and I plowed on. I can see it now, but then I couldn't. I was very close to his family and we had already started building a house together. It was my first house and I was so excited that I decided at that moment that I was going to go ahead with this wedding. "If it doesn't work out, I can always get a divorce," I said to myself. That was my logic! What a sad, self-centered, rebellious person I was, ever trying to control my own world.

We got married and our life together began ... well, it began to unravel. After barely one year, I was struggling to keep all my balls in the air. I would come home to balance the checkbook, clean the house, mow the yard, and then go off on another trip. We were constantly fighting and I was exhausted.

It was obvious that he was not ready for marriage. He was still enjoying partying and playing with his friends, and my traveling was no help. On one trip, hurt and frustrated, I met a guy whose words found a way into my heart. We started a relationship, and that affair was the end of my second marriage.

I can look back and see how out of balance I really was. If I had been in balance, his words would not have derailed me.

Nevertheless, I had again failed at another relationship. I was hurting everyone around me though I wasn't trying to. I had never worked through my abandonment issues. In fact, I needed a complete transformation, but I didn't know it yet.

Despite the emotional scars that divorce leaves behind, I was excited about my future. I was ready to move forward, to run and not look back. I was free. I was free to leave before someone else abandoned me.

That's pretty twisted logic, and if you've ever been there, then please take time out to deal with your abandonment issues. Don't think that the I'll-leave-you-before-you-leave-me way of thinking is healthy, much less balanced. That will only perpetuate your hurt.

But that was my approach. I did not know that I was running away before I could be abandoned again. The burden of dividing my attention between my child-like husband and me was over. I could devote all my energies to myself, toward achieving my goals and reaching my potential.

As a nutritionist, my timing was ideal. After decades of drinking, smoking, and unhealthy eating, the acceptable norm in the United States was changing. Americans were finally waking up to the importance of health and nutrition. And I was ready for the challenge.

Free to close that chapter of my life and begin the march forward, I decided it was time to stop depending on others to make me happy. It was back to depending on me. I would control my own fate. I would look within and find the inner strength I knew that I had.

In order to achieve my goals and get where I wanted to go professionally, I knew I needed to move. There were too many memories and "skeletons" from my unsuccessful marriage to stay in the home we had built. I needed a fresh start, so I moved to San Antonio, about 100 miles south from where I was currently living. I felt confident I could use my connections with friends and family to begin elevating my career to the next level.

The only drawback in moving, of course, was the painful process of starting all over. I knew that in order to work as an independent nutritionist, I would need sufficient time to build up a client base, develop contacts, network across town, and more. I was open to other options in the nutrition field, but I could not count on having a nutrition-related job immediately upon arriving in San Antonio.

Fortunately, I had developed a friendship with the owner of a tile and granite company who was looking for an outside sales person. He offered me the job and I eagerly accepted it. Odd as it seemed to be doing something completely unrelated to the field of nutrition, I was grateful to have a job that provided a revenue stream during this time of transition. I purchased a beautiful home in an exclusive neighborhood. I felt this was an important and necessary investment for me. I needed my privacy. I didn't want interruptions. I wanted a "command center" from which I could plan, strategize, and map out my future. It was time for me to become the captain of my own ship, and I didn't need or want anyone else's help.

Sound familiar? Have you ever been there? If you had told me, "I don't think that believing you don't need anyone's help is walking in balance either," I wouldn't have believed you … but you would have been right!

Living as a "Lone Ranger" was not foreign to me. In retrospect, I think this is one reason why marriage did not work for me. I had serious abandonment issues. Deep down I feared more episodes of desertion. I think the rest of society shares my concern. Come on, nearly half of all marriages fail! There has to be some serious hurts and errors in our thinking to drive up such a bad statistic.

Or maybe deep down, I feared the pain of my spouse leaving me for another woman. The scars of abandonment from childhood had not yet healed, which meant that I could not risk enduring that pain once more.

The more independent I became, the less I liked the concept of marriage. It seemed to be the antithesis of who I was. Marriage is a partnership, a union of two people who bear equal responsibility for each other, but I tried it and it didn't work. (Never mind my bad logic, but that was what I thought. In truth, just because you try something and it doesn't work does NOT mean anything.)

I reached a point where I felt sympathy for those who were married. They said they were happy, but I thought deep down that they were weak. I was stronger than them, and I had a great sense of liberty that came from being the master of my own destiny. (Funny, isn't it, what you can say to yourself to justify your own inadequacies, problems, and guilty feelings?) When I moved to San Antonio, I begin dating my new boss, the owner of the tile shop. We genuinely enjoyed each other's company, and I was open to a relationship. Nothing had changed with regard to my self-sufficiency, but I recognized that a simple relationship/friendship with a man was a far cry from marriage.

I saw relationships as unbinding, noncommittal, and that's what I wanted. I wanted the best of both worlds. I welcomed the attention, companionship, and intimacy that came with a relationship, but without all the commitment. Marriage is constraining, I thought, and I was fine with what we had.

If you have ever had phrases like "Intimacy with no strings is best" or "Marriage is constraining" whispered into your ears, please recognize that these words are based in fear. They come out of a hurting heart, mind, and soul. What's more, I've learned since then that whenever a fear speaks to you, it's lying. Every single time!

So, much as I liked and possibly loved this guy, I would not allow things to move beyond friendship, intimate though it was. Anything more serious would not be conducive to my ultimate goals. I couldn't afford to allow any person or thing to inhibit my career path.

Within months, I was detecting a sense of momentum in my life. I had put my previous life behind me and I was reestablishing myself in San Antonio. I was actually doing pretty well as a tile salesperson, but that job was only temporary. Soon I would be among the city's most respected nutritionists. I could feel it in my bones.

I was exceedingly proud of myself for not quitting, as I easily could have. Through my many bumps, obstacles, detours, and years of college, I had made it. I had applied myself. I had emerged victorious!

At just 36 years of age, I was still young. I was pretty. I was confident. I wasn't just good, I was great … and I knew it! Fame and fortune were in the crosshairs of my future. I could feel it! I could taste it! What could possibly inhibit my rapid rise?

As a nutritionist, it was incredibly satisfying to know I could take care of myself. I would not allow a decline in my health because I had knowledge and expertise. How comforting this was for me. I was riding a wave and nothing was going to stop me.

George Orwell said, "Most people get a fair amount of fun out of their lives, but on balance life is suffering, and only the very young or very foolish imagine otherwise." I would soon come face to face with the truth of these words.

One cold morning in January, everything changed. I awoke, and lying there in my bed, I contemplated the new day and all I had scheduled. There were clients to meet and appointments to keep. As my alarm sounded, I stepped out of bed and headed toward the shower.

I never made it.

I wasn't in any discomfort or pain, but I sensed something was wrong as I collapsed on the ground. I did not know what had happened. "I must have tripped," I said to myself.

Using the doorframe as support, I pulled myself up, but this time I came crashing down like a felled oak tree. Now the room was spinning out of control and I was instantly stricken by an intense wave of nausea.

What on earth is happening to me? Am I having a heart attack? A stroke? A seizure?

As much as I tried, all my efforts to simply stand up were futile. I was alone and helpless on the floor. My cell phone was on the other side of the room, and that was too far to go. I couldn't call for help, as I lived alone in my beautiful home.

I felt panic! A sense of terror came over me. How could my life so instantly turn from normal to chaos?

My mind began rejecting everything that was happening. "This isn't real," I tried to convince myself. "This must be a dream. Surely, I am having a nightmare." I was sure soon I would awake and everything would be fine.

Unfortunately, I was wide awake and it was real.

Instead of figuring out some way to get help, my thoughts turned toward work and the many appointments I had scheduled for that day. How would I notify my clients I wasn't unavailable?

Silly to think about work when you are dying, isn't it? I had learned that in crisis situations, people don't think rationally. I wasn't thinking rationally! I kept thinking to myself, *What am I going to do? I have appointments and I can't even make it to the phone to start calling people.*

My thoughts then turned to rationalization, trying to convince myself this wasn't as serious as it seemed. "I probably have fluid in my ear, and I'm just going to take a sick day and by tomorrow it will all be over," I reasoned … and hoped.

In retrospect, that was one of the scariest, most difficult days of my life. There I was, a young, healthy nutritionist, lying on the floor, completely incapacitated. I could not sit, stand, or walk. Everything I did made the spinning, dizziness, and the nausea even worse.

As I tried to make it through the day, I became more anxious, longed for the next day, hoping, in my optimistic mind, that it would bring a return to normalcy.

After a good night's rest, my eyes opened. As I glanced toward my bedroom window, the morning sun was just beginning to peek through. I felt excited to start the new day and make up for all the lost time from the day before. I was eager to jump out of bed and put the darkness of the day prior behind me. Clinical Nutritionist Kay Spears was back in business!

But it was not to be.

As I swung my feet out of bed, I quickly realized this day would be no different. Back was the intense dizziness, the nausea, and the sensation that everything was out of balance. I could not get out of bed! I was terrified by the thought that my affliction was something far more serious than first realized.

I tried to be positive, and as each day passed, I believed that I was going to be fine. But I wasn't being honest with myself. Something was seriously wrong, and I would need help to overcome this. Little did I know that the ride I was on wasn't going to slow down anytime soon!

In fact, I was just beginning my journey to many healers.

Alison Stormwolf said, "Ask yourself honestly in duress…'What is my body trying to tell me?'" As a nutritionist, I counsel people all the time on how to get their bodies healthy again. I have worked with people with cancer and autoimmune disorders and I always have success getting people to feel better. That has always been my reward as a nutritionist.

Now, all of a sudden, I was the one looking for answers.

I researched my symptoms and it seemed that I had vertigo. I went to see colleagues, but they were not able to help me. It seemed I was not getting anywhere. I even made a trip to the emergency room after family members scared me into it. I have never liked emergency rooms. I see the emergency room as the place you go to if you want immediate symptoms treated, like a heart attack or a knife wound.

After several hours of waiting in the sitting area at the emergency room, we were finally called back. When the doctor came in, he asked a few questions, then said, "You have vertigo."

As the room was spinning around me, I laughed and said, "You are diagnosing me with vertigo! Vertigo is just a symptom, it is not a diagnosis!"

I demanded a MRI scan, but the doctor would not agree to it. He wanted to send me home with some drugs. As he left the room, my dad said to me, "Here you go again, always challenging doctors. Just listen to the doctor and let's go home!"

I really did not want to leave without a MRI because I wanted to rule out any neurological issues, but the little girl inside me wanted to please her daddy, so I agreed and we left. All the way home, I listened to my father tell me how difficult I was and how no one in my family could relate to me. That didn't help at all! His words hurt and I cried all the way home. He dropped me off at my house and I went straight to bed. Alone and wounded, I cried myself to sleep.

The next few months were a blur. They seemed endless. I went on several trips to healers in an effort to find out what was going on inside of me. I was not looking for a label for my illness ... I just wanted it to go away!

I got increasingly desperate and started seeking counsel from clairvoyants. I wanted to know if I was going to die and what avenue I was not seeking for my healing. I was doing positive imagery where I would see myself healed. Nothing helped. In all, I spent over $40,000 that year with any and every healer I heard about.

Keep in mind that I couldn't drive. Every time I needed to go somewhere, I had to call a friend to take me. Most of the trips to healers were miles away and took more than one day to receive treatments. It was taxing on me and my friends!

Desperation led to anger, but that didn't help. Having no answers left me confused. I was not getting anywhere. I just wanted my life back. That is the only way I can explain this feeling.

When you go from being a very healthy and active person to not even being able to leave the house or walk across the street, it is like your life has been taken from you.

I was starting to lose hope.

I felt like I was being punished by God. I knew I had a past that was not pleasing to God, so I began to see my vertigo as my punishment. As I have said, I always believed in God, but I never really understood what it was like to have a relationship with God.

In my desperate search for answers, I started to admit that my life was not really as balanced as I thought it was. My issues that I never addressed had not gone away just because I ignored them. I was facing reality, inch by inch.

Looking back, I really think our bodies will tell us when we are not in balance, and my vertigo was screaming "IMBALANCE!" so loudly that I couldn't help but hear it.

My life was out of balance in so many ways. I had a lot of financial debt, especially with my house. I was always working and stressing about it, for the mortgage and related expenses were more than I could afford. I was also constantly adding other debt to my one-person salary. On top of that, I was still struggling with my trail of bad relationships. I had two failed marriages, an affair, other hurtful relationships, and a current relationship that was not healthy. What's more, the abandonment issues with my parents hummed as a constant background noise that never seemed to leave me alone.

As the final "cherry" on top, I went around believing that I was in control and that I could control my own life. What a joke!

I truly felt it was payback time. God was going to make me pay!

It was during this time of self-examination that I went to see a chiropractor who had been known to help people with vertigo. I had actually known him for several years, but had never gone to him about my vertigo. When I was taken into his office, I started going through my symptoms and what needed to happen and how awful it had all been. I wanted him to listen to me and not just decide my treatment without hearing what was going on.

He looked at me and smiled. Then he put his hands on my shoulders and said, "You are not being punished and God loves you very much."

Wow! He must have turned on the faucet because I started crying uncontrollably right there in his office. In my family when I was growing up, tears were a sign of weakness, but I sat there and cried and cried. I couldn't stop!

When I left his office I felt so tired, but it was a good tired. I felt free on the inside. Something was happening, and it was on that day that things began to change.

That very same day, I set up an appointment with a certain counselor across town and she ended up being my mentor and helping me find the real Healer, Jesus Christ.

As soon as I stepped away from my symptoms and I realized I was not being punished, my symptoms started to subside. I decided I had to focus on all the imbalances in my life so I could get physically balanced.

How ironic is that?

Now, years later, I cannot tell you how satisfying, freeing, and exhilarating it is to really walk in balance. Trust me, this is a balance you want, in every way, shape, and form!

Nutrition

"Let food be your medicine and medicine be your food."
> *— Hippocrates (377-460 BC), the "Father of Medicine"*

The principle of nutrition is extremely important. When we do not eat right, we do not feel good. When we do not feel good, we cannot master any of the other principles of balance effectively.

Hippocrates, the father of medicine, said, "Let food be your medicine and medicine be your food." How powerful is that! Yet we are so under-nourished and way over-medicated. If we just got back to the basics and started eating more vegetables and less processed foods, we would be in a much better place.

I counsel people all day long on nutrition. Eating right is the hardest thing to do. Everyone is so busy and, conveniently, there seems to be a fast food restaurant on every corner. Preparing food from a can or box has become a way of life.

Food Is Emotional

Since there are so many emotions tied to food, sometimes I function more like a psychologist than a nutritionist. People come to see me who truly want to make a difference in their health, but they simply cannot break the bondage of food.

I really want to establish some new theories I have on the whole emotional aspect of eating. I promise you will learn some steps to help you eat properly, so bear with me while we get some issues out of the way first.

Theory Number One: **Eating is emotional —**
we must all eat!

We can quit drinking alcohol if we have a drinking problem. We can quit smoking (although it is hard) and never touch a cigarette again.

The problem with food is we must eat! Eating in our society is the focus of everything. We eat to celebrate, we eat when we are stressed, we eat when we mourn, and so on. As children, our parents rewarded us with ice cream and candy when we were good. All this explains the pathway for food being tied to all of our emotions.

It's a battle!

How do we solve this problem? Well, it takes a lot of reconditioning the mind for adults, and it will take adults committed to setting a different reward system other than food to break the cycle for our children.

Theory Number Two: **Our flesh wants us to do
what feels good at the time!**

In my personal experience, I've found that my flesh
wants what my flesh wants. For example, I want something that is not healthy for me because life is too short
and I should be able to enjoy myself, right?

But the truth is my metabolism gets all messed up and
then I start eating things I would not normally eat. To say
the least, I have to really fight my flesh. It is a true battle.

I emphasize "flesh" because our flesh always wants us
to do what feels good at the moment. Afterward, we beat
ourselves up because we did something we did not want
to do. I have to win this battle by self-talk. I have to say lit-
erally, "Flesh, you want what you want, but I'm not going
to give in because that does not serve me in a healthy
way." It isn't that I can't have it, but rather that I choose
not to have it.

Poor Health as a Nation

Now let's get down to business. Our nation is in poor
health, however I think we are recognizing the heath
crisis and the new "New Plate" Diet, formerly the
Standard American Diet, will be easier to understand
that half of our plates should be fruits and vegetables
and the other half is lean meat and whole grains. In my
opinion, the Standard American Diet contributed to the
fact that in the year 2000, approximately 125 million
Americans had chronic conditions and 61 million had
multiple chronic conditions. Today, 78% of each health

dollar is spent on chronic conditions. No discrimination exists here, for people of all incomes and races are afflicted with chronic diseases.

And get this, Americans have tripled their portion sizes since the 1950s! You go to a restaurant and the servings are enough for three people. Pasta servings are frequently three cups or more, which adds up to a whopping 600 calories. We all know that the more food that is in front of you, the more food you will eat.

How do we solve this problem?

You can solve this problem by incorporating a thera-peutic lifestyle that includes eating the right foods in the right portion sizes. Eat 4-6 meals per day, increase high fiber foods like vegetables and fruits, increase lean proteins and healthy fats, eliminate trans fats and simple sugars, and no eating after 7 p.m.

By doing these things, you will support blood sugar metabolism and feel great!

Lots of Small Meals Per Day

Let's talk about eating 4-6 meals per day. Eat every two to three hours, and eat smaller meals rather than eating three huge meals a day. If you are camping and you do not put any logs on the fire, what happens? You won't have a fire for the campsite. But if you put too many logs on the fire, you will snuff the fire out.

Our metabolism works the same way. If we eat too much at one time, our body can't metabolize our food quickly enough. We get this surge in insulin, which can be a fat storage hormone, and then one hour later, we crash. Conversely, waiting four hours between meals can cause us to crash. By the time we eat again, we are starving and then we make bad choices.

Eating every 2-3 hours can include things as simple as having a small snack such as an apple or a handful of almonds.

Proteins

Next, let's talk about why protein is important. Protein is important for growth and regeneration of all cells. It helps maintain healthy blood sugar levels, helps lower glycemic response, helps prevent insulin resistance, helps weight loss, improves the immune system, is good for satiation, and is important for muscle building.

It is important, however, that we do not eat too much protein and that our protein is lean meat like chicken, turkey, fish, and organ meats. Yes, I said organ meats! One of the reasons so many suffer vitamin D deficiencies is that we are not eating organ meats anymore. Organ meats are packed full of vitamin D and vitamin A. Doctors are finding that their patients are extremely deficient in vitamin D and it is a very important nutrient to prevent diabetes, cancer, and improve the overall immune system. Vitamin D and vitamin A should be in balance and if we want to balance these nutrients out, the simplest way is to eat more organ meats.

Use high quality soy (what I mean by high quality soy is fermented soy, not processed, pasteurized soy that most of us are consuming in our store-bought soy products). Whey protein is a good source of protein. Cottage cheese, legumes, nuts and seeds, and eggs are also good quality proteins. Protein is essential, even if you are vegetarian.

If you are vegetarian, you want to be a healthy vegetarian. Some of the unhealthiest clients I see are vegetarians. Many of them eat lots of chips and pasta and don't include any protein sources. You can still combine foods to get protein.

I always tell my clients to eat 9-12 ounces of protein a day (three ounces is the size of the palm of your hand). You should always include a protein with a healthy carbohydrate to help blood sugar metabolism. I enjoy a protein smoothie in the morning made with a high quality whey protein powder. In a blender, I mix four ounces of kefir or yogurt with protein powder and frozen berries. This makes a high protein, nutrient-packed smoothie that starts my day out right.

Carbohydrates

Let's move on to carbohydrates. Carbohydrates provide calories and energy. Carbohydrates are mainly sugars (simple carbohydrates) and starches (complex carbohydrates found in bread, pasta, beans) that the body breaks down into glucose.

We need to choose carbohydrates that produce small fluctuations in blood glucose and insulin levels. These carbohydrates are called low glycemic carbohydrates. Examples of low glycemic carbohydrates include most vegetables, except for carrots and sweet potatoes (these are still foods we want to eat, but in moderation). Also, most fruits (except for banana, pineapple, and watermelon) are good sources of low glycemic carbohydrates.

It is important to look for breads and pasta that are 100% whole grain because these grains are lower glycemic carbohydrates. They should also be consumed in moderation.

If you follow these guidelines for carbohydrates, you will have sustainable weight loss and good health. The traditional food guide pyramid includes too many carbohydrates, which is one reason we are experiencing an increase in obesity, along with insulin resistance, a precursor to diabetes.

An example of a well-balanced lunch or dinner would be steamed veggies, brown rice, three ounces of chicken, and a small sweet potato.

Fats

Finally, let's talk about fats. Fat has been given a bad rap! We need good fats. Our brains are 67% fat. We need good fats for our brains to be able to function properly. Good fats help control inflammation in the body and we need good fats to make hormones in the body, like progesterone, estrogen, and testosterone. These are just a few of the hormones we get from good fats.

Good fats are important for satiety. They help us stay satisfied so we don't crave more food. And good fats are important for aging skin. I look at people who participated in the no-fat diet back in the 80s and their skin is wrinkled and aged. Fats keep our skin supple and they keep the elasticity strong.

Good fats include olive oil, coconut oil, real butter, ghee, fish oil, and flax oil. Fats we want to stay away from include lard, margarine, vegetable oil, soybean oil, and canola oil. I like to cook with coconut oil because it has a higher heat point than olive oil. This means that coconut oil will not become rancid. It tastes wonderful in stir-fry dishes. Olive oil is also a good cooking oil. For salad dressings, I like to use flax oil. Flax oil has a nutty taste and is good with apple cider vinegar.

I want to spend some time talking about the margarine and butter topic. Let me explain what margarine is. Margarine makers start with cheap, poor-quality vegetable oils, such as corn, cottonseed, soybean, safflower, and canola oils. These oils have already turned rancid from being extracted from oil seeds using high temperature and high pressure. Rancid oils are loaded with free radicals that react easily with other molecules, causing cell damage, premature aging, and a host of other problems. A solvent called hexane is used to remove every last bit of oil from the source. Hexane is actually known to cause cancer!

The next step in making margarine is hydrogenation, which is a high temperature process that turns the solution from a liquid into a semi solid. Hydrogenation is where hydrogen molecules are forced into oil molecules through the use of high heat, high pressure, and toxic catalysts such as nickel. At the end of the hydrogenation process, margarine does not smell good and is gray in color. The next step is that the margarine is bleached and deodorized, so artificial flavors and dyes are added. Interestingly enough, rats will not have anything to do with margarine. Humans are the only ones who will eat it! We get fooled by the logical reasoning that our media uses to trick us.

Trans fats found in margarine are much more harmful than saturated fats found in butter. Trans fats cause heart disease, obesity, diabetes, cancer, and other degenerative diseases. Saturated fats have been used for thousands of years. In China they use lard, in Europe they use butter, and in India they use ghee. When you go to the tropics, coconut oil is the main oil used for cooking. Heart disease and obesity has actually gone up when people started using more vegetable oils and other harmful trans fats like margarine.

I mentioned earlier how the rate of deficiencies in vitamin D has gone up since we have cut organ meats from our diet. The same goes for cutting butter and using margarine. Butter is made by collecting milk from cattle and goats. The cream is separated from the milk and it is continuously mixed until the cream is turned into butter! That is it! All the nutrients are intact, no nickel, hexane, or artificial dyes are added. Am I saying go eat a pound of butter a day? No, I am not. I am saying that we need to get back to eating our food the way God intended.

A Menu that You Can Use

Now that I have covered some of the basics, let me share with you a sample menu that will cover all the areas I talked about. It includes a protein or fat with every meal to support blood sugar metabolism. This sample menu includes vegetables and fruits. I have incorporated a raw food several times throughout the day, which helps your body get the enzymes it needs; enzymes we are often missing because we cook our food. I have also included snacks throughout the day.

You will notice that food is eaten every two to three hours. This supports blood sugar metabolism and increases the metabolism. Remember when I said that if you do not feed a campfire fuel, that it will go out? Well, by eating small meals throughout the day, we are letting our bodies know that they are getting food for fuel so they never think they are starving.

I also want to add that breakfast, which means "break fast," must be eaten one hour after getting up in the morning. Your body has been fasting and if you do not eat breakfast soon after awakening, then you are slowing down your metabolism.

This menu plan is just a sample. It is not a "one size fits all." Everyone has different caloric needs based on activity and height and weight. I put together customized programs after really looking at someone's body composition, using a machine that tells me the individual's resting metabolic rate. In this sample menu, however, you can see how to combine food and what types of food to eat.

Sample Menu

7:00 a.m.	4 oz. kefir, scoop of protein powder with berries
9:00 a.m.	10-12 raw almonds
12:00 p.m.	Green leafy salad with avocado, 3 oz. of chicken and vinaigrette dressing
2:00 p.m.	Small apple
4:00 p.m.	¼ cup of hummus with celery sticks
6:00 p.m.	3 oz. of fish, medium sweet potato and steamed veggies

What Happens to Your Body

It takes about a week of eating like this before your body physically stops craving sugar. This is because it takes about a week to get the blood sugar stabilized in the body. Once you have beaten the physical cravings of your blood sugar trying to get balanced, the rest of the battle is mental.

The mental battle includes the two aspects I mentioned earlier. We must fight our emotional aspects of eating. Once we understand why we are doing what we are doing, then we are able to master the emotional part of eating.

The biggest battle is the plain torture of the flesh, which is constantly saying, "I want what I want because I want it." This is where prayer can help tremendously. We can ask God to help us deal with our flesh. Once we renew our minds and look to food as our friend and not our enemy, we have won the battle.

I always have clients telling me that they feel deprived when they are out with friends. They often feel they have to say, "I cannot have what you are eating because I am on a diet."

That is where I step in right away and explain that you should never tell yourself that you can't have something. Instead, you must tell yourself, "I choose not to have that because it does not serve me in a healthy way."

The next thing clients often tell me is that diets do not work. I reply, "This is not a diet, it is a lifestyle change. This is how you should be eating for the rest of your life. And I promise that you can achieve this."

When we are eating right, we feel better. When we feel better, we can be more efficient in our daily activities, we will be happier in our relationships, and we will be able to fulfill our God-given purpose. Are those not good enough reasons to eat healthy?

When you master this principle, you will be able to sail through the rest of the principles and be on your way to achieving the ultimate goal of finding balance! When you have balance, nothing can stop you, and you will live this life with peace!

Questions to Consider:
- Are you getting enough vegetables?
- How many snacks per day are you eating?

From a Fan

My goal of weight loss is to "age" healthily. At the age of 51, I began to seek a common sense, scientific, and individualized approach to weight loss. I have tried a multitude of diets, including Weight Watchers, a program through which I actually gained weight!

In my search, I discovered Kay Spears' overall nutrition approach. It is a program that met all of my requirements: balanced nutrition, proportions, scientific (in that it included laboratory testing to determine the need for nutritional supplements), bioelectrical impedance analysis (a body-fat measurement device), and individualized (the program plan was developed just for my nutritional and caloric needs).

Over the 8-week program, I lost 20 pounds, but most importantly, my total cholesterol dropped to 187, which allowed me to come off a cholesterol lowering medication. As I lost weight, I had more energy to exercise. This approach is not just a diet but a lifestyle change!

P.S. I weighed myself this morning and am down to 198.8 lbs. I walked a 10-mile hike today at Government Canyon State Park! Thanks!

— *Betty I.*

From a Fan

Nutrisystem, Optifast, Weight Watchers, South Beach, Atkins, diet pills, starvation, shots, etc. These are just some of the ways I have tried over the last thirty years to lose weight. My knee joints were arthritic from the weight burden, sugar levels inching upward, cholesterol numbers elevating. My last ditch effort was to take the referral of a friend of mine to go see Kay. I had never, over the years, successfully lost more than 25 pounds on a diet. After each diet attempt, my weight would return, almost always with additional weight added on. Kay ran some tests on me, referred me to a physician for additional testing, and our journey began. She has guided and continues to guide me on what and how to eat healthy. I never, in all my years, expected to be able to lose over eighty pounds without starving myself. I have been told in fact that I sometimes am not eating enough! Kay and I have been a team for over two years. It has been a slow climb, but I have managed to maintain my weight loss. I continue to see Kay on a weekly basis. I weigh in and we commensurate on my eating status. This journey has not been an easy one and it is not over yet. Kay has been my mentor, my guide, my cheerleader, and my friend. I would highly recommend Kay to anyone wishing to improve their health through nutritional counseling. I have been blessed to be her client.

— J. Lowry C

3

Supplementation

"In order to change, we must be sick and tired of being sick and tired."

— *Author Unknown*

Supplementation is an important step in the quest for balance. I wish I could say that our food supply provides all the nutrients we need to be healthy and balanced, but that is not the case. In addition, we do not eat a variety of foods. We are all creatures of habit and we eat the same things all the time, and usually this does not include nutrient-dense foods.

Nutrient-dense foods are foods that have a high nutrient to calorie ratio, for example, strawberries. One cup of strawberries contains only 150 calories, but they also contain 3.5 g fiber, 86 mg of vitamin C, and 26.9 mcg of folate. Sweet foods that are high in sugar, such as candy bars, donuts, and cookies, are not considered nutrient dense because they do not have significant amounts of vitamins and minerals. This is why they are referred to as "empty" calories.

The Soil Isn't What It Used to Be

Dirt is not just dirt. It is the soil in which our plants grow, and its nutrient value is becoming more and more depleted. As a result, nutrient-dense foods are not as nutrient dense as they should be. Vegetables, grains, and fruit are now being grown on land that no longer contains sufficient minerals. (You can read a great article on this topic at: http://www.state-journal.com/news/simple_article /4815484?page=0.)

In the State Journal article, written on January 16, 2011, it stated,

> In less than 20 years the parts-per million content of iron in tomatoes went from 1938 to under 5; spinach has gone from 1584 to less than 31.2. The mineral content in corn in the 1920s was 5%; today it is less than 1%.

Wheat has dropped in protein and mineral content by more than half. Recent studies that compared the mineral content of soils today with soils 100 years ago found that agricultural soils in the United States have been depleted of 85% of their minerals.

Today, more than 80% of the diseases that plague this planet are rooted in nutritional deficiencies. Research has shown that without adequate nutrition (especially minerals), people develop chronic health conditions. More and more nutritional studies have linked many of today's most prevalent, life-threatening chronic diseases like diabetes, heart disease, stroke, obesity, high blood pressure, macular degeneration, bone loss, and dementia to nutritional deficiencies. So if we think we do not need supplements, think again.

Important Manufacturing Information

Now that we have established the value and need for supplementation, it is important to know how to look for quality supplements. Finding supplements can be extremely overwhelming.

I will start by saying that there are no Food and Drug Administration regulations on supplements. When looking for a supplement, it is important to look for products that are GMP (Good Manufacturing Practice) certified, which means they are part of a quality system that covers the manufacture and testing of active pharmaceutical ingredients.

The FDA states the purpose of GMP regulations is to implement systems that assure proper design of supplements and that monitor and control the manufacturing processes and facilities. GMP certified products are higher quality and have third-party companies that do assays. These third-party assays are independent from the manufacturing company and they assure that the nutrients and the amounts are compliant with what the label says.

Important Forms of Nutrients

Since there are not any FDA regulations on supplements, a lot of manufacturers will use cheaper forms of nutrients in order to generate greater profits. This means that anyone can sell you a vitamin. The problem is that this is not better for consumers. Companies will use glues and binders that are not absorbed by the body. When a vitamin is heated to high temperatures and bonded with glue binders, the nutrients are not only destroyed in the process, but the glues cannot be absorbed by the body.

There is much to know about how nutrients are combined and why and when to take them. This is why the Internet can be dangerous sometimes. It is important to work with a nutritionist because supplements can cause more harm than good if not used properly. Nutritionists spend a lot of time learning about nutrients and their purpose.

There are hundreds of nutritional health supplements available and this can be extremely overwhelming. The best supplements are those that can be readily absorbed and used by the body. It is also important that the supplements you choose be free from dyes, allergens, and artificial preservatives and that they are the proper forms of nutrients your body can utilize.

Do we all need the same nutrients?

It is important to know that throughout our lives, we are all subject to different nutrition deficiencies and that we are all biochemically different. This means that we all do not need the same supplements. There are some basic nutrients that we should take, which I will discuss, but it is always important to work with a nutritionist to find out what specific nutrients you may be deficient in.

When you get your blood work done by the laboratory, a nutritionist can accurately detect abnormalities in your blood chemistry. A doctor will be looking for gross disease abnormalities, but for a nutritionist, the goal is to provide education for understanding optimum levels of health to prevent and reverse many dysfunctions in your body. By analyzing your blood work using optimal ranges, a nutritionist can identify nutrition deficiencies that are occurring in your body and provide therapeutic supplementation based on your individual needs.

There is a level of basic supplementation that applies to everyone. Again, it is important to know that you personally could have some deficiencies that require additional supplementation. I do believe, however, that no matter what that we should incorporate a few supplements as part of our arsenal.

Fish Oil

I believe that we all should be taking a good quality fish oil (EPA/DHA). Fish oil is a type of fat that cannot be manufactured by the body and needs to come from the diet.

One of the benefits of EPA/DHA is improved cognitive function. Our brains are 60% fat. The Myelin, which is the protective sheath that covers communicating neurons in the brain, is composed of 30% protein and 70% fat. This is why good fats are important for our overall brain health. After all, our brains are our computer systems that operate the rest of our bodies.

EPA/DHA is important for infant neural system development. DHA (docosahexaenoic acid) and AA (arachidonic acid) are both very important in the development of the brain and eyes. During pregnancy, the mother supplies the developing fetus with these fatty acids, and she continues to provide this important brain food to her infant through her breast milk.

Clinical evidence supports the role of EPA/DHA in decreasing blood triglycerides and decreasing LDL cholesterol (the bad cholesterol). EPA/DHA shows clinical evidence to reduce blood pressure. Research shows less frequent thrombosis in patients taking EPA/DHA and there is clear evidence of the benefits of decreasing atherosclerosis. *The Lancet* (1999) reported, "In one study of 11,324 coronary heart disease sufferers, who were already taking standard therapies for heart disease, the consumption of 1.0 gram per day of EPA/DHA reduced risk of sudden cardiac death by 45% and overall mortality by 20%."

Essential fatty acids include omega-3 fatty acids and omega-6 fatty acids. Alpha-linolenic acid is a member of the group of essential fatty acids called omega-3 fatty acids, so called because they are an essential dietary requirement for all mammals. Most seeds and seed oils are much richer in the omega-6 fat linoleic acid. Linoleic acid is also an essential fat, but it, along with the other omega-6 fats, competes with omega-3s for position in cell membranes. The primary sources of omega-6 fats are corn, soy, canola, safflower, and sunflower oil; these oils are overabundant in the typical diet, which explains our excess omega-6 levels.

You should avoid or limit these omega-6 oils. Omega-3, meanwhile, is typically found in flaxseed oil, walnut oil, and fish. By far, the best type of omega-3 fats are those found in fish. That's because the omega-3 in fish is high in two fatty acids crucial to human health, EPA and DHA. These two fatty acids are extremely important in preventing heart disease, cancer, and many other diseases.

It is clear that omega-3s have major health benefits for everyone. The problem is that only 27% of the population ever eat oily fish. This is why we need a good quality fish oil supplement.

Supplementing with high quality fish oil is very important because of the mercury issue. It is crucial to look for GMP certified fish oil. GMP certification will mean that the fish oil has probably gone through a distillation process to remove the mercury and other harmful contaminants. Also, GMP certification has official guidelines for bottling. When you open a bottle of fish oil, it should not smell fishy. It should actually smell clean. When it has a strong odor, chances are that the oil could be rancid. Companies should be nitrogen flushing the fish oil so it will not become rancid. I recommend 3 to 4 grams of fish oil a day.

I also recommend taking fish oil capsules with enteric coating, which means that the fish oil will not be released until it reaches the small intestine. This keeps you from experiencing that fish repeat taste in the back of your throat. The enteric coating on the fish oil also increases the absorption rate by 300%. The total amount of EPA/DHA is more important than the ratio. Most of the fish we eat is higher in DHA than EPA, whereas most of the fish oil we consume is higher in EPA than DHA.

It seems that krill oil has become the choice for a lot of consumers trying to get as many of the benefits from the EPA/DHA as possible. The problem with krill oil is that it is providing phospholipids, but we do not have a shortage of phospholipids in our bodies. Krill oil only has a small amount of EPA/DHA, which is what we are lacking. The research shows that we need high dosages of the EPA/DHA, and this is found in the fish oil.

Alpha-linolenic Acid

Alpha-linolenic acid is a minor component in tissues. Seed oils are the richest sources of alpha-linolenic acid, notably those of rapeseed (canola), soybeans, walnuts, flaxseed (linseed), perilla, chia, and hemp. Alpha-linolenic acid (ALA) is also obtained from the thylakoid mem-branes of the green leaves of broadleaf plants (the mem-branes responsible for photosynthesis). Greens, therefore, and animals that eat greens, are often a good source of ALA.

Studies have found evidence that ALA is related to a lower risk of cardiovascular disease. However, the mecha-nism is still unclear. The body converts ALA into the lon-ger chain fatty acids eicosapentaenoic acid (EPA) and docosahexaenoic acid (DHA), which is fish oil. You would also need to take about 20 to 40 grams of flax seed oil to deliver the EPA/DHA that the body ultimately needs.

Multivitamins

A good multivitamin is my next recommendation. Multivitamins should be from a whole food base. You should not use synthetic forms of nutrients. Our important nutrients should be from a diet of thirteen organic compounds and nineteen inorganic elements that the body needs for proper cell function. Our bodies cannot create these nutrients, which means they must come from our diets.

An optimal multivitamin will go beyond the typical "essential" nutrients and address those other nutrients that are conditionally essential. It will also contain antioxidants that have been shown to have a positive impact on health. Nutrients have a complex interaction with each other and nutrients must be supplied in balanced doses. It is important to understand that certain vitamins compete with others for absorption and can actually create deficiencies in other areas. This is one of the many reasons that it is important to take a good supplement that meets the GMP certification for quality.

Nutrients cannot be delivered to the body if they are not in their proper form. For instance, most minerals are not readily absorbed in their elemental form (i.e. the mineral by itself). They must be bound to an organic compound (chelated) or citric acid in order for the stomach's enzymes to effectively ingest and break down the nutrient. Companies tend to use the cheapest form of an ingredient, even though it may not be the optimal form for the body to utilize.

Scientists use the term bioavailability to measure what's absorbed by the body versus what's wasted. Unfortunately in ordinary multivitamins, a great deal of the nutrients don't benefit the body at all because they are not bioavailable. The big issue is that it is hard to determine bioavailability by reading labels; they only show what is in the multivitamin, and that does not give you any idea how much is bioavailable.

Many ordinary multivitamins were made using inexpensive processes and rely on additives. These processes can destroy the nutritional value of the supplements or render them unrecognizable to the body. Again, in order to make sure you are taking a high quality multivitamin, you should make sure you are working with a health practitioner who can provide you with the best quality and individualize the multivitamin that is right for you. The second option is to make sure you look for the GMP certification for a pharmaceutical grade supplement.

The final test is you! You should feel an improvement and if you are not, then maybe you need to switch your multivitamin. I am a big fan of Multigreens, because they are whole food based. Multigreens is a choice product for those who need more than just a regular multivitamin and mineral supplement. Multigreens provide highly absorbable micronutrients along with specialty nutrients and a proprietary blend of fruits, vegetables and enzymes to offer you a superior level of nutritional support. Although no supplement can replace a healthy well-balanced diet, the comprehensive nutrition provided in multigreens can be an excellent choice for picky eaters who do not always consume a balanced diet. Most greens supplements are in the form of poor tasting powders, leading to difficulties with personal consumption. In addition, many of these formulas do not provide a complete vitamin and mineral core. I like Premiere Multigreens because of its unique choice of powder or capsule and its nutrient rich superfood formula.

- 3300+ ORAC (Oxidation Reduction Absorbance Capacity) per serving (equivilent to 8-9 servings of fruits and vegatables).
- True multifaceted "Super Food" product in capsules.
- Proprietary blend of 15 different fruits and 16 different vegetables.
- Proprietary blend of 10 different enzymes including brush border enzymes to support small intestinal heath and proper digestion and absorption of dietary macronutrients.
- Numerous flavanoids, antioxidents, botanicals and green foods to supply a broad range of micronutrients.
- Supports heathy body PH.

Taking a superfood supplement, along with incorporating a lifestyle change consisting of eating nutrient dense foods like vegetables, fruits, nuts, and beans, would be the perfect multivitamin combination. I believe that if your food is right and you take a superfood supplement, along with a good quality fish oil, vitamin D, probiotic and fiber that you are covering your basic nutrients.

I am not saying that we never need additional supplements. Sometimes, our bodies have been so depleted over time that we create deficiencies that eventually start creating symptoms and illnesses. There is a time and a place for additional supplements.

Vitamin D

There has been tremendous research in the field of vitamin D. The findings are astounding! We now know that vitamin D affects almost every organ system in the body. Research has linked vitamin D deficiency to cancer, heart disease, diabetes, high blood pressure, kidney disease, fibromyalgia, chronic fatigue, osteoporosis, arthritis, lupus, M.S., asthma, thyroid diseases, dental problems, and depression.

Vitamin D is a steroid vitamin, a group of fat-soluble prohormones, which encourages the absorption and metabolism of calcium and phosphorous. We require ten to fifteen minutes of sun exposure at least twice a week, if not more on the face, arms, hands, or back, without sunscreen with a greater than 3 UV index for adequate amounts of vitamin D. Longer exposure results in the extra vitamin supply being degraded as fast as it is generated.

There are factors that keep us from getting adequate amounts of vitamin D. If you live far from the equator, your sunlight exposure will be less during many months of the year. As we age, we do not tend to go out in the sunlight as much. If you live in an area that is cloudy, you will not be getting enough sunlight. The color of your skin could limit your vitamin D absorption. Fair skinned people synthesize vitamin D from exposure to the sun more readily than darker complected people. Increased melanin in the skin of dark complexioned races impedes the absorption of sunlight and hence impedes the synthesis of vitamin D.

Vitamin D facilitates the absorption of calcium. The reduced serum levels in dark-skinned people residing in northern climates could lead to increased bone related disorders, especially bone fractures, due to reduced calcium absorption and osteoporosis.

It is very important to ask your doctor to test your vitamin D levels. Supplementation is dependent on a baseline test. The proper test for vitamin D levels is 25-hydroxy vitamin D. This is the most accurate way to measure how much vitamin D is in your body. The 25(OH) D test should not be confused with a test for 1, 25-dihydroxyvitamin D. The levels of 1, 25 (OH) 2 D do not typically decrease until vitamin D deficiency is severe. So the bottom line is that you could already be deficient in vitamin D, but if you get the wrong serum test, you may not know you are deficient.

Serum concentrations of 25(OH) D are reported in both nanograms per milliliter (ng/mL) and nanomoles per liter (nmol/L). (1 ng/mL = 2.5 nmol/L). The test measures the vitamin D circulating in the blood and not that which is stored in other parts of the body.

In 2007, a group of vitamin D and nutrition researchers published an editorial arguing that we should strive for vitamin D blood test results of 75 nmol/L (30 ng/mL) or more….and that 400 IU/day of vitamin D did little to help us reach this level. They also stated that approximately 1,700 IU of vitamin D are needed daily to raise blood levels from 20 to 32 ng/mL. (Vieth R, Bischoff-Ferrari H, Boucher BJ, Dawson-Hughes B, Garland CF, Heaney RP, et al. "The urgent need to recommend an intake of vitamin D that is effective." American Journal of Clinical Nutrition, 2007;85:649-50.)

The Vitamin D Council recommends that people take an average of 5,000 IU a day, year-round, if they have some sun exposure and possibly more if they have little or no sun exposure. The Council suggests that the further you live from the equator, the darker your skin, and/or the more you weigh, the larger vitamin D dosage will be needed to maintain optimal blood levels.

I believe your vitamin D levels should be 60 ng/mL. If you are below 30 ng/mL, it will take time to increase these levels up to 60 ng/mL. This is why it is important to have your vitamin D levels monitored throughout the course of therapeutic dosages to get your vitamin D levels up.

Your body can produce about 20,000 IU of vitamin D per day with full body sun exposure, about 5,000 IU with 50% of your body exposed, and as much as 1,000 IU with just 10% of your body exposed. You can also supplement with vitamin D, but be sure to choose the right form of vitamin D supplement. The one you want is the natural vitamin D3 (cholecalciferol), which is the same vitamin D your body produces when exposed to sunshine.

Probiotics

I must include probiotics as a staple nutrient because of the astounding information I have learned over the years about microorganisms and the perfect balance they require.

Microflora is a group or colony of microorganisms present in a specific, localized location and is our friend throughout our lives. Without this micorflora, we would become ill and die within five years of birth. There are many benefits of microflora. They are vital in our digestion. We cannot absorb our vitamins without microflora. Microflora protects us from infection and microflora helps our immune systems say strong all the time. We have microflora in our oral cavity, our respiratory tract, gastrointestinal tract, genito-urinary tract, and our skin. We have "100,000 billion viable microbes in our intestines … 10,000 billion total numbers of cells in our bodies … 1,000 billion microbes on our skin" (Seroyal and Dr. Nigel Plummer).

If you think about 100,000 billion viable microbes in our intestines, that is about three pounds of living bacteria in the GI tract. There are roughly 600 types of bacteria, of which 20% are unidentified. Our microflora can be thrown out of balance due to poor diet, antibiotic therapy, stress, lack of sleep, infection, and aging. Wow!

Here comes the word balance again. Look how important balance is in our lives, our bodies, and our emotions! When we are out of balance and our body inside becomes out of balance, our microflora becomes out of balance as well. This causes a war in the body in which the good and bad bacteria fall out of balance and the bad bacteria wins! When this bad bacteria takes over, the body is not balanced and we open ourselves up to reduction in our immune system. We become sick and then we end up taking an antibiotic that causes the war in our microflora to become even bigger! The good bacteria is destroyed even further with the antibiotic and the bad guys continue to overpopulate!

This is why we need probiotics. Probiotics are live microorganisms that are important for getting the good bacteria back in the body to help balance out that important microflora. When these probiotics are given in proper ratios, the benefits are crucial in getting our immune system strong. In fact, a probiotic can help improve digestion, lower risk of infection, reduce severity of allergy symptoms, improve the immune system, and help us improve our nutrition by helping us absorb nutrients.

This is why a probiotic has become a must-take in my opinion. There are several probiotic products on the market. For a healthy individual, I would recommend a probiotic dosage of 25 to 30 billion strains for maintenance. If you have taken several rounds of antibiotics or you suffer from any health issues, you may want to consider a more therapeutic dose of 100 billion. The important strains to look for are Lactobacillus acidophilus, Bifidobacterium lactis, bifidobaterium bifidum, saccharomyces boulardi, lactobacillus plantarum, and Lactobacillus rhamnosus. These may sound like big words and they do big jobs in our colon.

It is also good to include kefir in your diet. Kefir is like yogurt, but it is fermented longer and has more probiotics than yogurt. The fermentation process is what creates the probiotic and kefir has a spritzy tangy taste. I always add it to my protein shake. If you cannot find kefir, then a quality Greek yogurt will be a good substitute because it tends to have more beneficial bacteria. I like the brand Fage. It is always good to get the yogurt plain because the ones that have fruit added usually have a lot of sweetener added. The plain is good in a shake or you can add stevia and cinnamon to make it sweet and just eat it as a snack.

These are just some basic nutrients we could all use on a daily basis to help supplement our diet. Again, I stress we are all biochemically different and we have different deficiencies in our bodies. I highly recommend that you work with a certified nutritionist who can help you determine your program.

Fiber

Fiber supplementation is extremely important. Colon cancer is the second leading cause of death from cancer. This is partly because we don't eat foods that contain enough fiber and nutrients. For this reason, I think a good soluble and insoluble and why it's important to have both.

Soluble fiber is "soluble" in water. When mixed with water it forms a gel-like substancce and swells. Soluble fiber has many benefits, including moderating blood glucose levels and lowering cholesterol. The scientific names for soluble fibers include pectins, gums, mucilages, and some hemicelluloses. Good sources of soluble fiber include oats and oatmeal, legumes (peas, beans, lentils), barley, fruits and vegetables (especially oranges, apples and carrots).

Insoluble fiber does not absorb or dissolve in water. It passes through our digestive system in close to its original form. Insoluble fiber offers many benefits to intestinal health, including a reduction in the risk and occurence of colorectal cancer, hemorrhoids, and constipation. The scientific names for insoluble fibers include cellulose, lignins, and also some other hemicelluloses. Most of insoluble fibers come from the bran layers of cereal grains.

Since dietary fiber is found only in plant products (i.e., nuts, whole grains, legumes, fruits and vegetables), these are essential to a healthy diet.

I like UltraFiber Plus because it contains both soluble and insoluble fiber and most brands on the market don't contain both. It is a pure, gluten free dietary fiber supplement.

Questions to Consider:

- How do you know if you are taking supplements that are right for you?
- Does your fish oil smell funny when you open the bottle?

From a Fan

I heard Kay Spears speak at an event about taking control of your health and what she said made me want to come see her. My first visit with Kay was all about fact finding. Kay spent a lot of time going through my history, looking over blood work, and discussing testing that she wanted to do to look at neurotransmitters, adrenals, and hormones. I learned so much on that first visit. Once all the results were in for all the testing Kay did, she put together a customized program based on my individual needs.

I had already started feeling better from the nutrition program that was designed for me, but once I started taking the supplements that Kay recommended for me, I really started to see an improvement in how I felt. I was sleeping better and I had much more energy.

Kay's approach is to look at the whole person and not about treating symptoms. After one year of working with Kay, I went back to my doctor for a follow up on my dexa score, which had showed bone loss in the past. My dexa score showed improvement in my left hip and improvement in my spine. In fact, the doctor said that I am now almost in normal range!

I highly recommend Kay Spears.

— Sally K

From a Fan

This year has been a year full of blessings and wow, what a journey for me. Three and a half years ago, my husband and I started trying to begin a family. The more time went by, the more concerned we grew that we might not be able to start a family of our own. I went and saw my regular OB/GYN. He was so optimistic. He had me try a couple of rounds of Clomid (a fertility medicine), which my body did not respond to, and the more I read up on infertility, the more I recognized the acronym of PCOS.

I asked my doctor about it and he confirmed for me that my problem could very well be Polycystic Ovarian Syndrome (PCOS), which meant my body was not producing enough of the hormone level to make me ovulate. It took a while to settle with me, but I knew I was in the right hands.

He recommended that I see a Fertility Specialist. From the moment I walked in, I knew I was in the right place. They comforted me from the moment I stepped foot in the office. He, too, confirmed that PCOS was most likely the culprit of my not being able to get pregnant.

I tried fertility medicines, diets, and medications to help induce ovulation, as well as acupuncture. It was just so stressful, so I gave up for a while and just dieted to lose weight. As they say, if you lose 10% of your body fat, it has been known to spur on ovulation.

A few months later, I was pregnant. Yes, that's right, on my own without any help. The only problem was that I found out about my pregnancy in the emergency room of the hospital. I was having an ectopic pregnancy. A week later, my doctor removed the baby and my left fallopian tube.

My husband and I were devastated and happy all at the same time because I went from not being able to ovulate to becoming pregnant and losing my baby in a matter of a week. I pondered how overwhelming this was for us.

I withdrew into myself for a couple months and stayed away from family, friends, and kids. I had a friend who was concerned and brought me two books to read regarding infertility and the story of one woman's journey through an ordeal similar to mine but very different in other ways. One thing stuck with me throughout both readings and that was if I can't take care of myself, how could I ever expect God to bless me with a child to care for?

It was then that I took my health and nutrition to heart. I discovered an entire world I had never really taken time to learn about. It intrigued me. I sought help from a nutritionist on the referral of my doctor and has that ever been a blessing.

I started with Kay Spears of Nutrawise and recognized how great I really felt after only three weeks of changing what I ate. At this point, it was all about ME! I continued with the diet regimen that Kay provided for me and because I was so determined and so regimented, it paid off.

I am not saying it was an easy task the first few weeks, but did it ever enlighten me on what the body really does and how it really responds to the goodness of healthy foods! I lost about 2 lbs. per week and a total of 15 lbs. in about six weeks.

It was then I decided to do more for myself and go ahead and finish out my college degree so I had to take a physical education course. Well, I had always heard that yoga was a great exercise to do when you're trying to get pregnant and even during your pregnancy to help make your delivery easier, so I went ahead and signed up for a semester of beginner fitness yoga. I thought I'd get credit for my degree and help my body get in shape for pregnancy.

My journey through my doctor, my specialist Kay Spears, and now my yoga instructor has turned out to be the best therapeutic journey I could have ever gone through for myself. It not only enlightened me about the mental and physical benefits of nutrition and exercise, but it has also shown me the many spiritual benefits that can play a part.

I can now say that in this last 16 weeks, my curiosity and reason for being so intrigued about my health has given me the biggest blessing of all. I am now pregnant and in the second trimester of my pregnancy. Baby and mom are happy and healthy. Yes, I had a few bumps in the road to get to where I am today, but it goes to show you that if you want something bad enough, your tenacity and strength to achieve your goals will pay off in the end.

My thanks go out to Northeast OB/GYN, RMA of Texas, Nutrawise, and San Antonio College. These companies should know what a true asset each has been to my husband and me over the last several months.

Thank you!

— Cami G.

Exercise

*"By increasing oxygen, you can bring your
body's metabolic process into balance."*

— R. Dunham

George Burns (who lived to be 100) used to say, "If I
knew I was going to live this long, I would have taken better care of myself!" Let's not let that be our epitaph!

Physical activity is one of the most important things
you can do to enjoy a longer, healthier life and it is
required for balance in our lives, both physically and mentally. Being physically active helps you feel good and helps
you get more enjoyment out of life.

We often think of exercise as a way to look good. Well,
exercise does help with that, promoting sustainable weight
loss and helping you achieve physical fitness. But the focus
here is living a life of balance, so I am going to focus on
how exercise is going to help you stay balanced.

Exercise helps prolong your life, improve your mood,
achieve metabolic balance internally, strengthen heart

and blood vessels, increase bone density, and decrease risk for disease. ("Dis-ease" is a state when the body is out of balance.)

Get Healthy

Our heart is a muscular pump and it beats 100,000 times per day, that's 35 million times per year! Our heart also promotes oxygenation of tissues and delivery of nutrients and it promotes removal of waste products.

I think these are all good reasons to keep our heart balanced. Studies show that when we increase our exercise, we decrease heart disease, hypertension, insulin resistance and diabetes, arthritis, depression, cancer, and osteoporosis.

It is important to build muscle, because muscles use blood sugar for fuel. Exercise helps transport blood sugar into the body cells and it keeps blood sugar and insulin in a healthy range.

Three Types of Fitness

There are three types of fitness that will help keep you balanced. They are as follows:

Aerobic

Cardiovascular exercise is important because it supplies oxygen to your muscles. This includes walking, hiking, swimming, cycling, rowing, and running. Aerobic activity is great for metabolic balance, it uses fat and glucose for fuel, and it tones the cardiovascular system. It is important to do this type of exercise most days for 30 to 60 minutes.

Of course, I do work with clients who have health issues or injuries so it is important to modify this type of exercise accordingly. Some of my clients with specific restrictions use a rebound mini-trampoline for aerobic exercise. The mini trampoline is about 3' in diameter and 9" high. It is safe, easy to use, and effective.

Strength Training

Strength training is important because it increases lean body mass and improves basal metabolic rate. It is important to exercise the muscle until it is fatigued and to make sure that you are eating enough to support building muscle. It is vitally important that you eat enough of the proper foods and calories to sustain muscle building. This does not always mean that you need to eat more protein.

If your goal is to lose fat and maintain lean body mass, you would need to do strength training at least two times per week. If your goal is to increase lean body mass, you would need to train three to four times per week.

Flexibility

Flexibility is huge for balance. This is where even most athletes do not spend enough time. We lose flexibility and agility with aging as our muscle fibers shorten and our joint connective tissue weakens. When we do stretching exercises, this lengthens the muscle fibers, strengthens tendons and ligaments, and prevents injuries.

Stretching is also mentally relaxing. It is important to stretch five minutes before any exercise session and after. It is also important to keep these points in mind while stretching:

- Go slow - gradually stretch muscles
- Don't bounce - this may cause tears
- Don't curve spine - keep back straight
- Hold stretches for 5 - 30 seconds
- Stretch for at least 5 minutes after exercising

Remember, lean muscle mass is critical for long-term health, but muscle mass naturally decreases as we age. Adults lose 3% to 5 % of muscle mass per decade, and the decline accelerates to 1%-2% per year after age 50. If you exercise, the muscle mass can increase at any age. That is great news!

Muscle keeps us strong and it contributes to balance and bone strength. It is important to incorporate exercise to keep us balanced physically, mentally, and spiritually.

Questions to Consider:

- Are you doing any weight training to help keep your bones strong?
- Are you stretching every day?

Water

"Nothing is softer or more flexible than water, yet nothing can resist it."

— *Lao Tzu*

Could you be chronically dehydrated? That may seem like an odd question, but many people are chronically dehydrated and they never even realize it.

You are probably wondering how being dehydrated has anything to do with living a balanced life. Well, they are related, and in a big way. You can live longer without food than you can without water.

Water Is Essential to Life

Lack of water causes depression and it has a huge effect on brain function. Our bodies require at least eight glasses of water per day, and more during exercise, illness, and hot weather. People often think that even if they don't actually drink water, that they are getting enough by drinking coffee, tea, soft drinks, juice, or beer. Unfortunately, many of these beverages have a diuretic effect, encouraging the body to excrete water through urination rather than retaining it.

Think about a grape versus a raisin. The grape is plump, full, and juicy, containing natural water. The raisin is small, dry, and shriveled, and its water is gone. Although a grape in dehydrated condition is still a good and useful fruit, the human body, when dehydrated, does not function at its best and may be at risk for many ailments.

Consider:

- The body is composed of nearly 75% water.
- Water is required for many of the body's essential functions.
- Water is utilized as a solvent. It also provides a means to transport nutrients, hormones, and other elements.
- Water is essential for maintaining cell structure.
- Water is necessary to maintain proteins and enzymes. The process of maintaining proteins and enzymes is very important for the body to function efficiently.

On a side note, water is mentioned over 722 times in the Bible as a cleanser of our spirit

When You Are Low on Water

Chronic dehydration can lead to a loss or decrease in many bodily functions and may ultimately result in disease. Contrary to popular belief, dry mouth or thirst are not the first signs of dehydration. If you wait until you are thirsty, your body is already dehydrated. It takes about two hours for anything you drink to have an effect on your body's hydration level. By the time you feel thirsty, you are two hours behind!

When your body is deprived of water, a water rationing system takes effect. Histamine, a neurotransmitter, becomes active and redistributes water throughout your body. The order of circulatory priority is the brain, lungs, liver, kidneys, and glands, and then comes the muscles, bones, and skin. During periods of dehydration, histamine ensures that these vital organs have enough water to function properly.

If water is under supplied, it must be taken from within your body. Chronic dehydration can cause histamine to become excessively active. This may result in symptoms that may be mistaken for other disorders, such as allergies, asthma, dyspepsia, colitis, constipation, rheumatoid arthritis, and chronic pain in various parts of the body, like migraine headaches.

Dehydration

There are several signs of dehydration.
1 — Dyspeptic pain

Dyspeptic pain, which can range from simple heartburn to gastro-esophageal reflux disorder (G.E.R.D.), may be one of the early signs of dehydration. During the early digestive process when food enters the stomach, hydrochloric acid (HCl) is secreted to activate the enzymes to break down the proteins found in meat and dairy. The acidic contents of the stomach (chyme) are then pumped into the small intestine by passing through a valve (the pyloric sphincter).

The acidic contents must be neutralized before they damage the intestinal lining. The pancreas is responsible for secreting the bicarbonate ions that neutralize this acid. A large amount of water is required to produce this bicarbonate solution. If sufficient water is not available, the digestive process may be delayed and food may remain in the stomach longer than necessary. Over a period of time, the stomach acid may rise and fall to enter the esophagus, which will produce the G.E.R.D. sensation.

Ideally, you should drink water 30 minutes before meals, during meals, and again two hours after eating.

2 — Joint pain

Joint pain is another possible complication of dehydration. The cartilage in your body, including your joints, is mainly composed of water. As cartilage surfaces glide over one another, some exposed cells become worn and peel away. New cartilage is normally produced to replace the damaged cells. Due to the lack of blood vessels in cartilage, water is needed to transport the nutrients required for maintenance and repair. Dehydration may increase the abrasive damage and delay its repair, resulting in joint pain.

3 — Asthma

Asthma and allergies can be another indication that the body has increased production of histamine. During chronic dehydration, the body will attempt to conserve water by preventing unnecessary water loss. A large amount of water is normally lost from the lungs as water vaporizes through expired air. Histamine, which also controls bronchial muscle contractions, may attempt to restrict water loss through expiration by constricting the bronchial muscles.

4 — Constipation

Another complication of dehydration can be constipation. When water is in short supply in the body, the colon will act to restrict unnecessary water loss through the stools. Colon muscles will contract to squeeze out and subsequently reabsorb water back into circulation. This can result in harder stools that are not only more difficult to pass, but may also irritate and weaken the walls of the colon, resulting in small pockets known as diverticuli. Since the water that the colon reabsorbs back into circulation is not clean water, the liver and the kidneys must filter it. This places additional strain on these overworked organs.

5 — Depression

Dehydration can contribute to feeling depressed. The brain requires the amino acid tryptophan to produce the neurotransmitter serotonin, which is subsequently needed to make melatonin. An adequate amount of water is required for tryptophan to be transported into the brain. Dehydration may limit the amount of tryptophan available to the brain. To complicate matters, the increased histamine levels may actually stimulate tryptophan's breakdown in the liver.

Re-hydration Required

Most of your body's water is found within the cells and the next largest source being the fluid surrounding the cells. If water is not replaced frequently, this surrounding fluid may continue to accumulate waste material and other contaminates. The pumps in your cell membranes may not work as efficiently because toxic water in cells can cause cellular damage or cell death.

You wouldn't bathe in the same bath water without first cleaning the tub and adding fresh water, so why would you allow your cells to be surrounded by toxic waste material?

Water is vital to good health and there is no substitute for water. However, years of chronic dehydration cannot be reversed overnight by simply drinking a couple of extra glasses of water a day. Rather, water intake should be gradually increased.

How do you know if you're drinking enough water? Your urine should be clear or lightly colored. Darker colored urine may be an indication that your kidneys are working hard to concentrate the urine.

What's In the Water?

Not all water is healthy water. Don't be tricked! Healthy water is water that has been properly treated to avoid contamination.

Nearly all municipal water supplies have chlorine and fluoride (a highly toxic bone poison that should be

avoided at all costs) added during water treatment, both
of which are detrimental to your health. Be sure and
obtain a filter to avoid ingesting chlorine and fluoride.
The other issue with water supplies in the U.S. is that
they also contain unhealthy arsenic levels that can cause
you health problems.

**There are several ways to obtain healthy water in
your home:**

- Avoid distilled water. Distilled water has the wrong
  ionization, pH, and polarization and oxidation
  potentials. Distilled water tends to leach your body
  of important minerals.
- Filter your water.

There are two main types of filters that I recommend:

- Carbon filters: These work well to remove impurities
  but may not remove fluoride. The GE Smart Water
  carbon filter was top rated in Consumer Reports in
  December 2002.
- Reverse osmosis: This type of system removes most
  impurities. I recommend the reverse osmosis system
  by Premier Research labs.

Avoid bottled water.

- There was a special aired on 20/20 talking about
  bottled water. Apparently, 40% of bottled water is
  just regular tap water. It is better to fill your stainless
  steel bottle daily with water from your reverse
  osmosis system. Pre-packaged water I do highly
  recommend is Mountain Valley water. They deliver

this water in glass bottles. Store your water safely. Avoid purchasing the one-gallon cloudy plastic (PVC) containers from your grocery store, as they transfer far too many chemicals into your water. The five-gallon containers and the clear bottles (polyethyl ene) are made from a much better plastic and will not give the water an unpalatable plastic taste.

- Overall, I recomend buying a stainless steel bottle for transporting water. Stainless steel bottles are BPA (Bisphenol-A) free, which is important because BPA has been associated with cancers and other health conditions. Stainless steel can be washed and rinsed, as opposed to plastic bottles that end up in the land fill. You also have less exposure to toxins and bacteria with stainless steel.

Questions to Consider:
- What color is your urine?
- How is your energy?

Sleep

"Sleep is the golden chain that ties health and our bodies together."

— *Thomas Dekker*

Sleep is the one area where we all seem to cheat. I can tell you this is the one area in which you may find yourself extremely out of balance. Sleep is a natural part of life, and while some people try to get by with as little as possible, packing their days and nights with activities, chores, work, and play, sleep is essential to health and to optimal performance every day.

A basic need of the human body, sleep is also a basic need of the human mind. Without enough sleep, our bodies and minds cannot function properly and we cannot achieve the goals we set out to do.

During sleep, our bodies take time to rejuvenate and our minds take time to work through problems, to explore themselves, and to rest. These activities are essential for your health and well-being.

Most adults need about eight hours of sleep every day. If sleeplessness becomes chronic, the consequences become more severe. Chronic loss of sleep over a period of time will seriously diminish your ability to perform work on the job or at home. Sluggishness, forgetfulness, lack of concentration, slower reaction times, and general malaise will begin to take over. This could result in accidents, injuries, and even behavior problems. Your enjoyment of life will decrease and other's enjoyment of you will decrease (because you will most likely be grouchy and lethargic).

Without enough sleep, your body cannot repair and replenish itself, and your mind cannot take the time it needs from the constant bombardment of the outside world to perform the tasks that it must during sleep periods. Our tendency is to create more tasks and more deadlines for ourselves, and we cut out sleep to get these done. If you are guilty of this, then please reconsider your sleeping habits.

Learn to Say "No!"

I think learning to say "no" is an important concept. It is important that we help others and that we do not just focus on our own lives, but we need balance in this. I counsel so many moms who are involved with their kids in every sport there is and who volunteer for everything they can. Why do they do it? Partly to show their kids how much they care, but also to show other moms how perfect they are. These are the moms who break down and end up on antidepressants.

Keeping up with the Joneses is the fastest way to have a nervous breakdown. The reason I am putting this issue in the sleep category is because I see moms going to bed later and getting up earlier to complete all the tasks at hand. I see businesspeople trying to make deadlines, so they stay at the office until midnight and then get up at 5 a.m. to finish their work. This is not how it is supposed to be.

Back in the old days when we did not have electricity or technology, people went to bed when it was dark and got up when it was light. Now we have computers, iPads we take to bed, and telephones that we never turn off, yet we wonder why we are so over stimulated, why we cannot fall asleep, and why we can't stay asleep through the night.

This used to be me. When my health was deteriorating, I had to make some changes in my life in order to get my balance back. All these changes were not easy, but I got my health back, and there is no price tag for that.

All these electronic devices can steal our peace and rest if we allow it. Addiction to them is certainly not helping our quality of life! If you want to get better sleep and have better health, turn off the TV, the cell phone, the computer, and the ebook reader.

On a practical level, if you have to get up at 5 a.m., then you should be getting ready for bed around 9 p.m. I know this sounds hard or you may think I'm crazy, but if you want to be balanced, you can't expect to shine on four hours of sleep!

Your life is what you make of it. You are in control of your schedule. If you have kids, you are in control of their schedules. You have to set priorities straight and make the type of life that is going to give back, not suck the life out of you.

You Make Your Own Choices

Let's face it, TV is nothing but doom and gloom at night anyway. The news is never positive and when we watch this negative stuff before bed, we end up having bad dreams or restless sleep. Turn off the electronics and read something calming, listen to peaceful music, meditate on positive affirmations, or read the Bible. These are all the first steps to creating better sleep, which will mean better health.

It is also important to keep your bedroom comfortable and dark at night. This will help you to sleep better. When it is really cold outside, I have tried wearing socks to bed, and that does help me fall asleep. Sometimes I cannot fall asleep because I have a lot on my mind. I started taking a pad and pen to bed and I write things down that pop into my head. Then I tell myself that I am going to deal with everything tomorrow. Then I do some deep breathing exercises to keep my mind off all the things I just wrote down. This helps me tremendously and I find that I am able to fall asleep instead of watching the clock. Limiting caffeine is also helpful for falling asleep.

I also found that if I was drinking too much water before bed, I had to get up several times during the night. Getting up frequently during the night disrupts our sleep cycle and creates a sleep deficit. Even though we think we are sleeping, we are not getting good quality sleep. Limiting liquids a couple hours before bed will help you stay asleep through the night. It is also important to avoid snacking before bed, especially on grains and sugar.

I have decided that I will not allow myself to have negative conversations or negative thoughts before bed. It was amazing how I had to work on this. Since evenings are our down time, we often get phone calls at night that are full of gossip or bad news. In addition, thoughts are more active at night because we are not focused on work or our errands. I make sure at night that I do not talk to people on the phone who tend to call with negative gossip. If I have negative thoughts, I quickly change my thought direction or distract myself with something else.

I think it is important to point out that we should not balance our checkbook, pay bills, or have discussions about finances right before bed. Worrying about finances is a sure way to lose sleep at night.

As you can tell, getting proper sleep is all about rearranging our schedules. We have to set up new habits. The latest study I read said that it takes 72 days to change a habit. It takes time to set up a balanced life, but I promise that it works and that you will be much happier and have much more energy if you implement some of these steps.

You may even find that you are able to eliminate your sleep medications and antidepressants.

Questions to Consider:

- Are you sleeping between the hours of 11 p.m. and 2 a.m.? This allows the liver to flush out toxins properly.
- Are you falling asleep right away?

Forgiveness

"To forgive is to set a prisoner free and discover that the prisoner was you."

— *Lewis B. Smedes*

The first step to finding balance in life is to embrace the critical component of forgiveness. As a Certified Clinical Nutritionist, I can say with certainty that it is impossible to be a healthy person as long as you harbor resentment toward others in your heart.

I'm not saying definitively that you do harbor resentment in your heart, I'm just saying that if you do, balance will be elusive. (And I know this truth personally!)

Forgiveness must be in your personal toolbox every day. The Bible tells us our world has been fallen since the Garden of Eden, and it doesn't take much to know, feel, and experience the fact that our planet is inhabited by imperfect people! Not a day will pass without someone offending us in one way or another. Even those closest to us, like our family and dear friends, are capable of committing grievous acts that deeply anger and offend us.

Often, it's those we love the most who inflict the most severe pain. We expect more from them in terms of their interaction with us, and they let us down. Throughout our lives, we can anticipate that people may mistreat us by lying, cheating, stealing, gossiping, or through countless other transgressions. And if we are humble enough to admit it, we know in our heart of hearts that we may do the same to others. We are all human, and unless we exercise forgiveness, we will remain stuck in the past and allow matters that should no be longer relevant to inhibit our present growth.

Forgiveness Required

When I say that balance and health are impossible without forgiveness, I fully recognize that forgiveness is one of the most difficult requirements of life. Long ago, English poet Alexander Pope coined the phrase, "To err is human but to forgive is divine." Indeed, forgiveness is essential...but though we are His creation, most of us are not willing to let go of the pain that someone has inflicted on us.

The problem is that the pain you harbor inside of you is only hurting you. The people you choose to be angry with are probably completely unaware that you are not forgiving them. They don't know. Only you know.

My grandmother used to say, "While you are home crying, they are out dancing." The people you are angry with are not suffering at all! They are out living life, while you are creating pain and suffering, and in the end this could turn into physical manifestations of disease.

Consider this example. I receive a call from a client who wishes to schedule an appointment on Friday and I am booked solid. I adjust my schedule so I can see her. On Tuesday, my client's child becomes intensely ill. The malady endures for several days and, in the process, my client completely forgets about our appointment and never calls me. Friday comes and my client doesn't show. This is the second time she's done this!

And me? I'M ANGRY! *I will hold this against her and will never forgive her!*

My Own Journey to Forgiveness

In my journey to finding balance, I ran smack into unforgiveness. It was an eye-opening experience. I did not have just one person I was not forgiving. No, I had a lot of people I needed to forgive, and that included myself.

When I started reading the book *The Spiritual Roots of Disease* by Pastor Henry W. Wright, I realized that I could not sit back and ignore this issue any longer, especially if I wanted to heal. I was desperate. If you told me I had to jump off a cliff and do somersaults, I would have done it!

I thought forgiveness would be easy, but boy was I wrong! It was the most difficult and longest part of my journey to healing.

First, I had to start with a list, a list of all the people who had harmed me in my life. I never thought my list would be so long! Then I needed to think about all the things each person had done to me. Instead of dwelling on all those bad things they did, I had to think about what had happened in their lives that might have caused them to act that way.

I started with my mom. She told me that she wished she never had me, chased me around the house with objects, all while screaming what a horrible child I was. How is someone supposed to forgive that? I was a child and she was supposed to be the adult. In addition to this, she abandoned me (and my brother and sister). She left to go to another state with her new husband.

With that reality, I stopped to think about how my mom was raised. When I realized that my mom was raised by deaf parents who basically used her to communicate with the world, when I realized my mom was sent to her room for five days in the dark when she asked her mom why she was bleeding at 13, I could not help but weep and think that my mom was raising us the only way she

knew how. Right, wrong, or indifferent, I had to find forgiveness. I knew my mom would never be the nurturing
type, but I knew in her own way, she loved me.

Next, I had to deal with two different incidents of
men trying to take advantage of me. I actually dropped a
case against a man who was trying to get me, as a child,
to perform acts from the book, *The Joy of Sex*. I was so
scared that I could not face this man in court. As a child,
I felt like it was my fault. I had to learn to forgive him,
and men in general, and realize that not all men intended
to abuse my body.

I had to forgive my dad. I realized through counseling
that I had several issues about feeling inadequate that were
attributed to my father.

Go Deep to Get Free

Just when I thought I was clear on all of my forgiveness issues, I was invited to attend the Trinity Program,
which is a program designed for a small group of people
with similar issues where you confess your sins to one
another. In my group, there were ten strangers, and we
spent a weekend together, learning how to forgive and
learning that our self-worth did not come from anyone
except God.

I went into this group on the cocky side. I told myself
that I had done all the work to achieve forgiveness. After
all, I had been to several of these soul-searching programs
before. I would always sit back and watch everyone else

open up and move forward. I did the work in my head and kept to myself. I was in control and I was not going to air my dirty laundry in front of anyone.

Instead of focusing on myself, I attended the Trinity Program under the guise that I was there to learn something that I could take back to my clients. That attitude was clinical enough for me to feel safe and secure ... but I soon realized I still had several unresolved issues.

On the second day of the program, I was a little nervous. Previous workshops never included sitting around a round table with ten strangers and confessing all our sins! All the things in my life that I was ashamed of ... all the things I wished I could take back ... they were all swirling around in my mind.

As the people talked, it got closer and closer to my turn. I could feel my throat closing up. My heart was beating so rapidly and loudly that I could barely hear the others speaking. I didn't know why I was reacting so negatively to this group. I had nothing to work on, or so I thought. Finally, it was my turn.

At that point, I was ready to get up and flee, to run and never look back. I did not know these ten strangers, and they would never see me again. Instead of running, I started by saying, "Well, I have already worked on my forgiveness issues, so I am just going to go down my list here." I had my list and I read through several bullet points. Suddenly, when I mentioned one little thing on my page, I started crying uncontrollably!

The one "little thing" was an incident when I was about 12 or 13. I was kissing a boy behind the bushes when my grandmother found me and called me a tramp. I ran away that day and ended up getting into a car with a complete stranger.I soon found myself in a bad situation that I could not control. The next day I found a payphone and called my dad to come pick me up, but I never mentally went back to that terrible day. I did not tell my dad and I completely blocked out the incident until that moment as we sat around the table.

As I was bawling, I remember thinking to myself, *Stop, stop!* Crying was a sign of weakness, as my dad used to tell us. The whole event was a total out-of-body experience that I cannot even explain. Afterwards, I remember walking to lunch with my new best friends! I felt tired and confused, but I also felt free! The Trinity Program allowed me to really free myself of unforgiveness and bondage that I had held on to for so long. I felt like I had a new beginning in life. I had just let my whole past go. Once again, the only way I can describe it is as being totally free!

Get Balanced

My point is that unforgiveness is the one thing that will keep you totally unbalanced. Forgiveness is balance between you and others. When you are able to let all that go, you can move on and focus on other things.

Pastor Henry Wright says, "The spiritual root to all disease is unforgiveness." I believe it! And if you want to live a balanced life, then you must get rid of any unforgiveness.

Join me in walking in freedom!

Questions to Consider:

- When you think of someone who has harmed you, do you feel angry or sad?
- Are you willing to reach out to someone you feel you have not forgiven?

Attitude of Gratitude

*"Gratitude helps you to grow and expand;
gratitude brings joy and laughter into your life
and into the lives of all those around you."*

— *Eileen Caddy*

Gratitude means thankfulness, gratefulness, or appreciation. It is a positive emotion or attitude in acknowledgement of a benefit that you have received or will receive.

Historically, gratitude has been the focus for several world religions. It has now become a mainstream focus of psychological research. Studies show clear changes in the immune system, brain, and heart when your thoughts are negative.

An attitude of gratitude is huge if you want to truly achieve balance in your life. You have so much to be grateful for and your situation can always be worse. It is imperative that you get up every day and give thanks and appreciate what you have.

Carolyn Leaf, a neuroscientist, explains how we are our own neuro "plastician." What that means is that we are able to change our brain chemistry with our thoughts. Carolyn has been researching the brain for years and she has found that we are all wired to love. Our thought process was never supposed to be wired for negative thoughts. Over time through our negative life experiences, we have developed negative thought processes. These negative thoughts are toxic and they cause too many chemicals to saturate the brain. The more negative our thought process becomes, the more toxic our brain chemistry becomes and the more we cannot shut off the negative thoughts. Sooner or later, we cannot even think positive thoughts anymore. Carolyn says that "87% to 95% of mental and physical illnesses are due to toxic negative thoughts."

Wow! I could not believe that! I knew negative thoughts were bad, but this showed me how much we are in control of our health and our destiny.

We Have the Power!

The brain is so powerful that we have the ability after a stroke to reroute the brain so that it can continue to function on its uninjured portion. This is amazing because when another part of the brain is trained to take over, you can fully recover from a stroke!

I have been thinking about psychopaths and what causes their brains to have such horrible thoughts that they actually lose their ability to have a conscience. One theory is the prefrontal cortex of the brain (that has to do with developing a conscience) is not working properly in psychopaths. But what do you expect when people are constantly in this state of negative thinking?

I truly believe that negative thinking is Satan's stronghold on many people. Satan can only get us by controlling our thoughts, and keeping us in this negative toxic state allows him to take over. Once these toxic thoughts consume us, we are not able to think positive thoughts anymore. Our negative toxic thoughts become actions and this is where I believe people who were once good will suddenly become bad.

A good example of this would be the Arizona event where a 22-year-old killed nine people and inured several more. Those who knew him in elementary school and high school said he was in a band and was happy, yet somehow he turned into a paranoid angry human being. His thought process turned negative somewhere. His negative thoughts took over becoming toxic and his toxic thoughts then turned into toxic actions.

I used to get up every morning thinking about all the things I had to do and all the things that were not right in my life. Those negative thoughts just made me think of more things in my life that were wrong. I was creating so much negative energy. Constantly wondering how I was going to accomplish more was one of the major reasons that I was so out of balance. This definitely triggered my physical manifestations of vertigo. My life was spinning out of control. My body was telling me exactly what was going on. Our bodies always tell us what we need to know when we are in tune with them.

Now, before my feet even hit the floor, I give thanks for all the wonderful things God has given me. I am thankful for the roof over my head, my car, and my job. I am extremely grateful that I have my health back. If you do not have your health, then life is not much fun.

I started carrying a gratitude rock in my purse. When I am having a bad day and it seems that nothing is going right, I simply reach for my gratitude rock. It makes me think about the positive things in my life and I smile. I feel much better. I feel an attitude of gratitude! As Brian Tracy exhorts:

> *"Develop an attitude of gratitude, and give thanks for everything that happens to you, knowing that every step forward is a step toward achieving something bigger and better than your current situation."*

In addition to the gratitude rock that I carry in my purse, I also started my own gratitude journal. Every evening I list the things I am grateful for. You can just start with five things. What I found is that as time went by, my list became longer and longer.

This journal is a personal history and it teaches you to become more grateful and more positive. We have to train our minds to be grateful. Our minds automatically want to think of the things we are lacking. When we train our thinking to right thinking, we begin this process with the words we say to ourselves. Every thought we think can create our realities. Usually our thoughts become words. I love these scriptures that sum up how important it is to protect our thoughts and our words:

"Death and life are in the power of the tongue, and those who love it will eat its fruit."

— *(Proverbs 18:21)*

"Pleasant words are like a honeycomb, sweetness to the soul and health to the bones."

— *(Proverbs 16:24)*

It is also important to visualize your success. I always tell my clients to visualize themselves as if they were already where they wanted to be. You must have a vision. Without vision, how do you know where you are going? When you lose your vision, you have no purpose and you get stuck. Life is constantly changing and your vision is constantly changing too. Your vision keeps you grateful and keeps your attitudes positive.

It is important to pray and ask God for inspiration and guidance. If your vision is aligned with God's plan for you, then there will not be anything that can stop you.

Our desires are usually God directing us to a purpose. We just have to be open to the wisdom. I will share with you one of my personal visions. I never ever thought I could write a book or be a public speaker, but God kept putting both of these action steps on my heart. I wanted to ignore it, but every time I turned around, I was being asked to do a public speaking engagement and people would ask me when I was going to write a book. It got to the point where I had to start taking the steps to become comfortable with speaking and writing. I joined Toastmasters to get over my fear of public speaking and once I took that step, things started to fall into place. I started lining up my vision with God's plan for me, and doors started opening.

Questions to Consider:
- Before you get out of bed, do you think about all the good things you have in your life?
- Are you helping those who are less fortunate than you?

Conclusion

I have given you the steps that are clearly important to keep you balanced in such a chaotic world. To ignore any of these steps is like baking a cake without all the ingredients. Chances are you will not have a cake.

As I mentioned in my personal story, I was a nutritionist, I was eating right, I was taking my supplements, I thought I had all the answers, yet my physical manifestation of vertigo led me on the search to find out what was wrong with my life. I thought I was in control, but I wasn't. I had to dig deep and learn more about my body.

As I really started focusing on myself, I could truly see what was lacking. All of this made me a better nutritionist because I started noticing that I could only take my clients so far. My clients would come in to see me and I would build a nutrition program, add some supplements, and then I would send them on their way.

When they would come back, I could see that I was making a difference, but it was not enough. Some things were missing. I realized I needed to spend time in all the areas. It was like a light switching on! My clients were coming back with better results, they seemed more at peace, and cellular changes were clearly taking place.

I chose to write this book because I want to get this information to anyone who is ready to receive it. I can change lives more by getting this book in people's hands than I can in counseling one on one. Life is demanding, our world keeps getting busier and busier, and we are mass-producing our food to keep up with the demands of the consumer. If we do not get back to some of the basics and take a few steps to balance our lives, we will be walking on a tight rope over Niagara Falls ... and the outcome is not going to be good.

The staggering statistics of adults and children who need antidepressant medications keep climbing. Approximately 1 in 18, or 14.4 million people in the U.S. experience depression. Approximately 4% of adolescents are seriously depressed. The problem is that we are over committing ourselves and our children. We put children in four different sports and we teach them to be over-achievers. We build our schedules so full, we cut out sleep and exercise. We are too busy to stop, drink water, or eat. We are so worried about all the things that are wrong in our life that we do not even see all the wonderful things around us. And we are so full of anger and resentment towards people in our past that we are paralyzed to move forward in love and forgiveness. We do not take time out to sit back and reflect. What about enjoying the sunshine, which can solve our huge problem of vitamin D deficiency? After a while, we snowball into a frenzy of depression and anxiety.

Now, more than ever, we need to stop and evaluate how we are handling life, and more importantly, how our families are handling life.

These steps that I have explained will change your life! The bottom line is that life is too short and our quality of life is too important to mess it up. In Italy, I learned *l'arte di non fare niente*. This is an Italian expression that translates as "the art of doing nothing." We say "killing time," but that has a negative connotation. We believe that we should always be doing something, but in Italy, it is *dolce far niente* — the "sweetness of doing nothing!"

Do we have to go all the way to Italy to feel like it is okay to enjoy doing nothing? This needs to change!

I wanted to share my story as part of this book because I wanted you to understand that I was lost. I thought I had it all together and I certainly did not think I needed anyone's help, including God's, in my life. I had several friends who were Christians and I had been to many churches. Most Christians drove me further away from God because I would watch how they acted, how they would dress up nice for church, but in the end they were not great examples of what God is supposed to reflect.

But I discovered that I needed God. God is unconditional love. He gives peace, forgiveness, and acceptance, and He always makes it all work out.

I laugh when I watch my dogs. They are always happy, they always love me, they are always at peace, they are so trusting, and they never wonder where their next meal is coming from. They are great teachers because this is how we should be in our lives. God simply takes care of our needs, if we let Him.

Today, I cannot imagine my life without God and I am so thankful for that chiropractor who put his arms around me and told me that God was not angry with me. That is what I thought, and that is what many people think. They feel that God is watching their every move and is going to punish them for everything they do wrong. They think that He is like Santa Claus, who doesn't deliver gifts to bad children.

My relationship with God is what taught me about the balance principles in this book. These principles saved my life, so I cannot keep the information inside. I want to share the good news with the world and let you know that life can be so wonderful! You can be empowered by knowledge. If you incorporate these steps, you can be on your way to a wonderful life.

Remember, you are in control. You have choices every day. What are you going to choose?

Weekly Meal Plans

Weekly Meal Planner #1

	Sunday	Monday	Tuesday	Wednesday	Thursday	Friday	Saturday
Breakfast	2 egg omelet, tomato, onion hot sauce	Protein shake, Kefir, Blueberries	Protein shake, almond butter	Protein shake, Strawberries, Cinnamon, ice	¼ c. oatmeal, Scoop of protein powder, Blueberries	Protein shake, Mixed berries, Kefir	¼ Quinoa Cinnamon Porridge. with coconut milk
Snack	Med. apple Almond butter	10 almonds	String cheese	2 hard-boiled eggs	Orange	String cheese	Protein shake, ice, and water
Lunch	½ whole grain sandwich hummus, avocado, alfalfa sprouts	Salad, 3oz of chicken, avocado, Braggs Apple Cider Dressing	Meat loaf Mixed salad with Braggs Salad Dressing	Homemade split pea soup, Salad with Bragg's vinegar	Mixed Green salad, avocado, chick peas, veggies, Bragg's vinegar	Spaghetti squash, meat sauce	Rotisserie chicken Sweet potato fries
Snack	Protein shake Blueberries	10 grapes	Blueberries 4 oz. plain yogurt, Cinnamon	¼ cup hummus, Celery sticks	4 oz. yogurt, walnuts, cinnamon, Stevia	8 pistachios	Strawberries
Dinner	3 oz. salmon med. sweet potato, steamed veggies	Meat loaf Green beans	Homemade split pea soup, Salad with Bragg's vinegar	Stir fry with veggies, coconut oil, chicken, brown rice	Spaghetti squash, meat sauce Mixed green salad with Braggs vinegar	Rotisserie chicken, Sweet potato fries	3oz steak Cauliflower Mashers, Salad

See alphabetized recipe index for preparation instructions

Weekly Meal Planner #2

	Sunday	Monday	Tuesday	Wednesday	Thursday	Friday	Saturday
Breakfast	2 egg omelet, tomato, onion hot sauce	Protein shake, Kefir, Blueberries	Protein shake, almond butter	Protein shake Strawberries, Cinnamon, ice	¼ c. oatmeal, Scoop of protein powder, Blueberries	Protein shake Mixed berries, Kefir	¼ Quinoa Cinnamon Porridge with Coconut milk
Snack	Med. apple Almond butter	10 almonds	String cheese	2 hard boiled eggs	Orange	String cheese	Protein shake, Ice, and water
Lunch	Green salad with hummus, avocado	Chicken fajitas with whole grain tortillas	Mango Salmon with basmati rice	Lamb with fried cauliflower	Grilled Chicken Pinto beans Sweet potato mashers	Tomato Cucumber salad	Dijon Pork chops and Sweet potatoes
Snack	Protein shake Blueberries	10 grapes	Blueberries 4 oz plain yogurt, cinnamon	¼ cup hummus, Celery sticks	4 oz. yogurt, walnuts, cinnamon, Stevia	8 pistachios	Strawberries
Dinner	Chicken fajitas with whole grain tortillas	Mango Salmon and basmati rice	Grilled leg of lamb with fried cauliflower	Grilled chicken Pinto beans Sweet potato mashers	Tomato Cucumber salad	Dijon pork Chops and Sweet potatoes	Barbeque chicken, homemade coleslaw

See alphabetized recipe index for preparation instructions

Weekly Meal Planner #3

	Sunday	Monday	Tuesday	Wednesday	Thursday	Friday	Saturday
Breakfast	2 egg omelet, tomato, onion hot sauce	Protein shake, Kefir, Blueberries	Protein shake almond butter	Protein shake, Strawberries, Cinnamon, ice	¼ c. oatmeal, Scoop of protein powder, Blueberries	Protein shake, Mixed berries, Kefir	¼ Quinoa Cinnamon Porridge with coconut milk
Snack	Med. apple Almond butter	10 almonds	Cantaloupe and cottage cheese	2 hard boiled eggs	Orange	Canteloupe	Protein shake, ice, and water
Lunch	Green salad with black beans, avocado	Chicken with Orange and olive, Basmati rice	Salmon with dill, Green salad with cucumber	Watermelon and Cucumber Salad	Spaghetti sauce and whole wheat pasta	Turkey Taco Salad	Curry Chicken, Brown rice
Snack	Protein shake, Blueberries	10 grapes	¼ cup hummus Celery sticks	Yogurt, blueberries, walnuts	4 oz. yogurt, walnuts, cinnamon, Stevia	8 pistachios	Strawberries
Dinner	Chicken with Orange and Olive Basmati rice	Salmon with dill, Green salad with cucumber	Chicken Strawberry Salad	Spaghetti sauce and whole wheat pasta	Turkey tacos	Curry Chicken, Brown rice	Red snapper, Cauliflower rice

See alphabetized recipe index for preparation instructions

Weekly Meal Planner #4

	Sunday	Monday	Tuesday	Wednesday	Thursday	Friday	Saturday
Breakfast	2 egg omelet, tomato, onion hot sauce	Protein shake, Kefir, Blueberries	Protein shake almond butter	Protein shake, Strawberries, Cinnamon, ice	¼ c. oatmeal, Scoop of protein powder, Blueberries	Protein shake, Mixed berries, Kefir	¼ Quinoa Cinnamon Porridge with coconut milk
Snack	Med .apple Almond butter	10 almonds	Grapes	Cantaloupe and Cottage cheese	Orange	Cantaloupe	Protein shake, Ice, and water
Lunch	Green salad with black beans, avocado	Salad with turkey patty	Stuffed Cabbage	Chili with corn bread	Vegetable soup	Lemon Salmon, Green Beans Almondine	Grilled Chicken Salad
Snack	Protein shake, Blueberries	10 grapes	¼ cup hummus, Celery sticks	Yogurt, blueberries, walnuts	4 oz. yogurt, blueberries cinnamon, Stevia	8 pistachios	Strawberries
Dinner	Turkey burgers, Sweet potato fries	Stuffed Cabbage	Chili with corn bread	Vegetable Soup	Lemon Salmon, Green Beans Almondine	Breadless BLT Wrap	Ground beef and cabbage

See alphabetized recipe index for preparation instructions

Recipes

ALMOND FLOUR MUFFINS
(LOW GLYCEMIC)

2 c. almond flour (almond meal)

2 tsp. baking powder

1/4 tsp. salt

1/2 c. (1 stick) butter, melted

4 eggs

1/3 cup water

Sweetener to taste -- about 1/3 c. usually works well -- liquid preferred

1 c. of frozen berries

1/4 tsp. vanilla extract

Preheat oven to 350 F. Butter a muffin tin. You can really do it with any size, but I'm basing the recipe on a 12-muffin tin pan. Mix dry ingredients. Add wet ingredients and mix thoroughly. Fill muffin tins about 1/2 to 2/3 full and bake for about 15 minutes. (Makes 12 Servings, Per Serving: 185 calories; 1 1/2 g. effective carbohydrate; 2 g. Fiber; 6 g. Protein.)

ASIAN PORK AND PINEAPPLE KABOBS

1 lb. boneless pork loin, cut into 1-inch cubes
3/4 c. teriyaki marinade, divided
2 c. pineapple chunks, about 1-inch diameter
1 red pepper, cut into 1-inch squares
4 green onions, cut into 2-inch pieces
1/2 c. bottled Thai peanut sauce (optional)

Place pork in self-sealing plastic bag and add 1/2 c. teriyaki marinade. Refrigerate 2 to 4 hours. Preheat grill to medium high. Thread pork, pineapple, red peppers and green onions onto skewers. Grill kabobs directly over fire, turning to brown evenly, for about 10 to 12 minutes or until internal temperature reaches 155 degrees. Brush kabobs with reserved marinade. Serve on a bed of steamed rice with peanut sauce, if desired. (Makes 4 servings, Per Serving: 260 Calories; Total 10g. Fat; 60mg. Cholesterol; 21g. Protein–Note: nutrition information does NOT include the rice or the peanut sauce.)

BARBEQUE SAUCE
(LOW CARB)

Dash of mustard
Splash of lemon juice
1/4 c. of 1 carb Ketchup or no corn
syrup ketchup
1/4 c. onion pureed
1 clove garlic pureed
1 tsp. chili powder
1 tbsp. white vinegar
1 tbsp. liquid smoke
1 tbsp. olive oil
1/2 tsp. black pepper
1 tsp. honey

Bring all the ingredients to a boil. Refrigerate for 2
hours then bring mixture back to a boil. Add barbeque
sauce when your meat has 10 minutes left on the grill. Do
not coat raw meat. Add sauce to one side then cook for a
few minutes, then flip it to the other side and add sauce.

BOK CHOY WITH BROCCOLI

1 lb. bok choy, about 1 medium bunch
1 lb. broccoli, about 1 large bunch
1/2 c. water
2 tbsp. oil
1 clove garlic, minced
1 tbsp. fresh ginger, grated
2 tbsp. soy sauce

Cut the stalks off the bok choy and cut into 1-inch pieces. Coarsely chop the leaves. Peel the broccoli stalks and cut into 1/4-inch pieces. Cut the broccoli florets into bite-size pieces.

In a large skillet or wok, bring 1/2 cup water to a boil. Add the bok choy stalks and the broccoli stalks and florets. Cover and simmer on medium-low heat until the broccoli is bright green, about 5 minutes. Uncover; cook on high heat until the water evaporates, about 2-4 minutes. Take the wok off the heat and add the bok choy leaves, oil and garlic. Put the wok back on the heat; cook, stirring often for 2 minutes or until the broccoli is tender-crisp. Add the ginger and soy sauce and toss well.

Do not freeze.

(Makes 6 servings, Per Serving: 67 Calories; 5g. Fat; 3g. Protein; 5g. Carbohydrate; 2g. Dietary Fiber; 3g. Net Carbs.)

BRAGG'S AMINO SALAD DRESSING

1/3 c. olive oil
1/4 c. lemon juice
1 tsp. Dijon mustard
Herbs and freshly ground pepper to taste
1 clove garlic, minced
1/4 Bragg's Liquid Aminos

BRAGG'S APPLE CIDER VINEGAR DRESSING

2 tsp. flax oil
4 tsp. of Bragg's Apple Cider Vinegar
Pinch of sea salt
Pinch of oregano

BREADLESS BLT

1/2 cup raw chopped tomatoes
3 slices bacon, cooked until crisp
then crumbled
2 tablespoons mayonnaise (regular)
Black pepper to taste
3 to 4 large leaves of green lettuce

Mix chopped tomato with crumbled bacon, mayonnaise, and a generous amount of pepper. Spoon mixture into the center of the lettuce leaves, and wrap in either a burrito or taco shape.

(Whole recipe: 362 calories; 5g. effective carbohydrate; 2g. Fiber; 7g. Protein. Note-This is not a great protein source; most of the calories (202) come from the fat in the mayonnaise.)

CABBAGE AND HAMBURGER

2 lbs. ground beef, cooked and drained
One head chopped cabbage.

Stir fry the cabbage with beef until tender then seasoned to taste.

(Makes about 8 servings. Per Serving: 215 Calories; 13g. Fat; 20g Protein; 5g. Carbohydrate; 2g. Dietary Fiber; 3g Net Carbs.)

CANTALOUPE SNACK

1/2 cup regular cottage cheese (can
substitute ricotta for one more gram of
carbohydrate)
1 medium wedge of cantaloupe
2 tbsp. flax seed meal

CAULIFLOWER MASH

"I Can't Believe It's Not Mashed Potatoes"

1 large head cauliflower
1 tbsp. olive oil
1/3 c. low-fat milk or coconut milk
Salt and pepper to taste
1-2 tsp. garlic powder (optional) or curry
powder and nutmeg (optional)

Cut cauliflower into 4-6 pieces and steam until cooked
but not overdone. Place in blender or food processor with
remaining ingredients and blend until the consistency of
mashed potatoes. Serve immediately and enjoy the unique
flavor.

CAULIFLOWER (FRIED)

1/3 c. tahini

2 cloves garlic, minced

1 tbsp. chopped fresh parsley

1/4 c. water

1/4 c. fresh lemon juice

Salt and pepper to taste

6 c. olive oil for frying

1 head cauliflower, cut into florets

Whisk the tahini, garlic, parsley, water, and lemon juice together in a bowl until no lumps of tahini remain. Season to taste with salt and pepper and set aside.

Heat oil in deep fryer to 375 degrees F (190 degrees C).

Fry half of the cauliflower florets in the hot oil until they turn golden brown, about 8 minutes. Drain on a paper towel-lined plate. Repeat with the remaining florets. Serve immediately with the tahini sauce.

CAULIFLOWER RICE

1 head cauliflower (or however much
you want)

For easiest and best preparation of this dish, three
pieces of equipment are very helpful:
- A food processor
- A microwave
- A covered (or fairly tightly coverable)
  microwave-safe dish.

Process fresh cauliflower until it is the size of rice,
either using the plain steel blade or the shredder blade.
Alternatively, you can shred the cauliflower with a hand-
held grater, or even use a knife, if you have the dexterity to
chop it up VERY finely.

Microwave the cauliflower in a covered dish. DO NOT
ADD WATER. Cauliflower absorbs water like crazy, and
the "granules" will become gummy. To keep it fluffy, just
let the moisture in the cauliflower do its work.

CHICKEN FAJITAS
(PER SERVING)

Grilled, marinated chicken
1/2 cup pepper and onion mixture
1 tablespoon salsa
2 tablespoons guacamole

Chicken Fajita Marinade

1/4 c. lime juice
1/3 c. water
2 tbsp. olive oil
4 cloves garlic, crushed
2 tsp. soy sauce
1 tsp. salt
1/2 tsp. liquid smoke flavoring
1/2 tsp. cayenne pepper
1/2 tsp. ground black pepper

In a large resealable plastic bag, mix together the lime juice, water, olive oil, garlic, soy sauce, salt, and liquid smoke flavoring. Stir in cayenne and black pepper.

Place desired meat in the marinade and refrigerate at least 2 hours, or overnight. Cook as desired.

CHICKEN WITH ORANGES
AND OLIVES

Preparation Time: 15 mins
Cooking Time: 45 mins

>   1/2 c. orange juice
>   1/2 c. white wine
>   2 tbsp. olive oil
>   2 cloves garlic, quartered
>   2 MAGGI Chicken Flavor Bouillon Tablets
>   2 small onions, thinly sliced
>   1 (3 to 4 lbs. total) fryer chicken, skin
>   removed and cut into 8 pieces
>   2 oranges, peeled, thinly sliced and cut
>   in half
>   1/2 c. sliced pimiento-stuffed green olives
>   Hot, cooked rice

Preheat oven to 400° F. Line large, deep baking pan with foil.

Place orange juice, wine, oil, garlic and bouillon in blender; cover. Blend until smooth.

Place onion slices on bottom of prepared pan. Place chicken pieces skin-side-up on top of onions. Pour sauce mixture over chicken (reserve 1/4 cup sauce for basting); cover with orange slices and olives.

Bake, basting occasionally with reserved marinade, for 45 minutes or until lightly browned and fully cooked. Serve warm with cooked rice. (Makes 8 servings.)

CHICKEN STRAWBERRY SALAD

1 lb. boneless skinless chicken breast,
grilled or broiled
8 c. lettuce, spinach, and/or arugula
(enough to fill a 2-quart mixing bowl)
2 c. sliced strawberries
1/4 c. sliced or slivered toasted almonds
(toasted pine nuts or sunflower seeds are
also good)
4 oz. feta cheese, crumbled (parmesan also
works well)

Toss the greens with about ¼ cup strawberry vinai-
grette or other oil and vinegar type salad dressing. Arrange
the rest of the ingredients on top of the greens. For meal-
sized salads, distribute between two plates or bowls.

GRILLED CHICKEN SALAD

For a delicious, nutritious and low-carb meal, try out
this grilled chicken salad recipe. It's easy to prepare and
the only cooking required is the grilling of the chicken. I
sometimes throw in some slices of Fuji apple if I have any
handy or a mixture of seeds such as sunflower, pumpkin
or sesame seeds.

2 free-range chicken breasts
3 cloves of garlic, crushed
Juice from one lemon
1/8 c. olive oil
5 romaine lettuce leaves, roughly chopped
5 cherry tomatoes, halved
1 ring of Spanish onion, roughly chopped
Chopped fresh chives for sprinkling
1/4 c. of extra virgin olive oil
2 tbsp. of white wine vinegar
1 clove of garlic, finely chopped
Sea salt & pepper

Marinate the chicken breasts in the fridge for up to 1 hour in lemon juice, crushed garlic, 1/4 teaspoon of salt, and 1/8 cup of olive oil.

Heat up the grill and then cook the chicken for about 10-15 minutes. The chicken is ready when you cut it and the juices run clear.

Meanwhile, wash and dry all the vegetables and then arrange them in a salad bowl with the feta.

To prepare the dressing, mix together the 1/4-cup of extra virgin olive oil, white wine vinegar and finely chopped garlic. Whisk with a fork to combine well.

Slice the chicken and then arrange on top of the salad. Drizzle on the dressing and then sprinkle on the chopped chives.

CHILI

2 lbs. of lean ground beef
1/2 onion
2-Alarm Chili seasoning kit
8 oz. can of tomato sauce
Sea salt

Brown meat and onion together. Drain the fat and then follow the recipe on the 2-Alarm Chili packets. You can make the chili mild or hot. Also, you can add beans if you want.

HOMEMADE COLESLAW

Head of cabbage
1/2 c. olive oil mayonnaise
1 tblsp. yellow mustard
2 tsp. white vinegar
Pinch of sea salt and pepper to taste

Grate the cabbage either with a grater or a food processor. Add white vinegar, yellow mustard, olive oil mayo, sea salt and pepper to taste. I like mine with a vinegar taste.

DIJON PORK CHOPS

1/4 c. red wine vinegar
2 tbsp. olive oil
2 tbsp. Dijon mustard
2 tsp. minced fresh parsley
1/2 tsp. minced chives
1/4 tsp. dried tarragon
4 boneless butterflied pork chops
(4 oz. each), trimmed
Additional minced chives, optional

In a small bowl, combine the vinegar, oil, mustard and herbs; set aside.

Grill chops, uncovered, over medium heat for 2 minutes per side for 1/2-in. thick chops (4 minutes on each side for 1-in. chops). Brush with mustard mixture and grill 2 minutes longer. Turn; baste and grill 2 minutes longer or until juices run clear. Sprinkle with chives if desired. (Makes 4 servings.)

GREEN BEANS ALMONDINE

16 ounce bag frozen French cut
green beans
2 ounces slivered almonds
4 tablespoons butter
Salt and pepper, to taste

Cook the beans according to the package directions
until tender-crisp; drain well. Meanwhile, in a small saucepan, sauté the almonds in butter over medium-low heat
until the nuts start to change color. Watch closely and stir
frequently. Remove from the heat as soon as you see that
the nuts are changing color. They will continue to brown
off the heat. Stir the almonds and butter into the hot green
beans; season to taste with salt and pepper.

Can be frozen.

(Makes 4-6 servings, Per 1/4 recipe: 222 Calories; 19g Fat;
5g Protein; 11g Carbohydrate; 5g Dietary Fiber; 6g Net
Carbs

Per 1/6 recipe: 148 Calories; 13g Fat; 3g Protein; 8g
Carbohydrate; 3g Dietary Fiber; 5g Net Carbs)

GRILLED LEG OF LAMB
(SERVES 4 PER LB. OF MEAT)

1 leg of lamb (boned and butterflied by butcher)
2 cups beef stock or red wine
2 tsp. poultry seasoning
1 tsp. salt
3 cloves garlic, cut in slivers

Mix ingredients and marinate for 12-24 hours in refrigerator. Grill over hot coals approximately 20 minutes on each side. Baste occasionally while grilling. (Per 3 oz serving: 173 Calories; 0g. Carbohydrates; 24g. Protein; 8g. Fat)

BAKED LEMON SALMON

Prep Time: 5 minutes
Cook Time: 45 minutes
Total Time: 50 minutes

This cooking technique is something of a miracle. The fish bakes at a low heat right on the platter you will serve it on. No pans to wash! You will know it is done when the fish flakes, but it doesn't change color as much because it keeps its moisture -- no more dried-out fish! And it is so flavorful!

2 to 4 salmon filets - about 1 lb.

2 - 4 tbsp. fresh herbs, chopped (thyme or
dill is nice, but anything you like is
probably good)

1/2 tsp. pepper

1/2 tsp. salt (add a bit more if salt is kosher,
or if fish is skinned)

1 tsp. oil, at most - you just need a very thin film

I first saw this technique used on a segment of Jacques
Pepin's TV show "Fast Food My Way". His preparation is a
bit fancier by removing the skin. This is not necessary,
unless you don't want the unsightly skin hanging around
your elegant buffet. The meat lifts right off the skin after it
is done. It is a good idea to run your hand over the filet
and make sure there aren't a bunch of bones, but frankly I
don't always do that either - I figure people can pick out
their own bones. If you do pick out the bones, it makes it
easier if you drape the filet over something convex like a
bowl - the bones stick right out when you position the fish
this way.

Heat the oven to 200 F (not a typo).

Chop up the herbs, and mix them with the salt and
pepper. I happen to have lemon thyme in my garden, and
it is my favorite for fish, but regular thyme or any herb
you like works fine -- even parsley. If you want to use
more herbs, that's fine. Sometimes I mix in a tablespoon
or so of sesame seeds.

Smear the oil on an ovenproof serving platter and put the fish on the platter. If the filet is skinned, put some salt and pepper on both sides, otherwise just put the fish skin side down and season the top. I usually run my oily hand from the platter, smearing over the fish so the seasoning will stick a bit better.

Bake for about 40 to 45 minutes, until the salmon flakes. You won't believe how good it is. (Three servings per pound: 230 Calories; 0 Carbs, 30g. Protein.)

MANGO SALMON

2 tbsp.. tamari or regular soy sauce

1 tbsp. minced fresh ginger

1 cinnamon stick (3 inches)

1 tsp. rice or cider vinegar

1 10-oz. bottle mango nectar

6 salmon fillets, 6-oz. each and 1 in. thick

1 tsp. olive oil

In a small saucepan, stir together all ingredients, except for salmon. Bring to boil, reduce heat and simmer uncovered for 20-25 minutes or until reduced to about ¾ cup. Pour mixture through a strainer and discard the solids. Return to saucepan and keep warm.

Brush olive oil on broiler pan and place salmon on pan. Broil 5 inches away from heat for 5 minutes. Brush salmon with mango mixture and broil 3 more minutes or until fish flakes with fork.

Serve immediately and garnish salmon with remaining mixture as desired. (Makes 6 servings, Per Serving: 309 Calories; 5.5g. Carbohydrates; 36.4 g. Protein; 14.5g. Fat. For smaller appetites, recipe will serve more with less calories.)

HEALTHY MEATLOAF WITH OATMEAL

1 large can tomato puree
3/4 c. Quaker oats
1 egg
1/4 c. chopped onion
1/2 tsp. sea salt
1/4 tsp. pepper
1 1/2 lb. lean ground beef

Preheat oven to 350 degrees. Combine all ingredients except ground beef. Mix well. Add ground beef, mix lightly but thoroughly. Press into 8 x 4 inch loaf pan. Bake 1 hour. Drain, let stand 5 minutes.

HINT: This is better when it's refrigerated then re-heated.

QUINOA CINNAMON RECIPE

One of my favorite breakfast recipes is the nutty cinnamon quinoa recipe.

- 1 c. low fat milk or coconut milk
- 1 c. water
- 1 c. of quinoa (well-rinsed)
- 2 c. fresh blueberries or strawberries
- 1/2 tsp. finely ground cinnamon
- 1/3 c. chopped pecans (or any nut that you prefer)
- 4 tsp. organic nectar

This is so easy to make, all you have to do is bring the milk, water, and quinoa to a boil in a saucepan over high heat, then reduce the heat to medium-low. Cover and simmer for 15 minutes or until most the liquid is absorbed.

Turn off the heat and set it aside for 5 minutes while covered. Mix in cinnamon and blueberries and top with the chopped nuts.

Drizzle with nectar and serve.

ROTISSERIE CHICKEN

Whole chicken (organic if possible)
2 c. of organic chicken broth
Fresh rosemary (stuff chicken with
fresh rosemary)
1 garlic clove
1/4 tsp. of sea salt

Put chicken in crockpot with remaining ingredients.
Cook on low for 8 hours.

KAY'S FAVORITE SMOOTHIE

2 scoops protein powder
1 c. plain kefir
1 tbsp. almond butter
1/2 c. of frozen berries

Blend until desired consistency.

GRILLED SALMON WITH DILL

Prep Time: 5 minutes
Cook Time: 10 minutes
Total Time: 15 minutes

I love this grilled salmon recipe - it's so easy and so delicious. It is one of those you can serve to guests. Don't be afraid to put all that greenery on the grill - it works fine.

Salmon filet(s) - try to get pieces that have
an even thickness (can use Salmon steaks if
you want)
Balsamic vinegar
1 bunch fresh dill (enough for up to 3 lbs.
of salmon)
Salt, black pepper, and olive oil
Oil with high smoke point for grill
(such as vegetable oil or spray)

Sprinkle balsamic vinegar and salt over Salmon.
Chop up dill. Drizzle enough olive oil over the dill to coat it - a tablespoon or so. Add black pepper and salt to the pile of dill and toss with your hands, then cover the fish with the dill.
The salmon should ideally sit at least half an hour before cooking, but it isn't essential. If it's going to be longer, put the fish in the refrigerator then remove half an hour before cooking. It can even marinate overnight.

Get the grill good and hot. If it's a charcoal fire, only put the coals under one side of the grill.

Oil the grill (I like to use paper toweling on tongs), and put the salmon on, skin side down.

If you plan to eat the skin, flip the filets after about 2 minutes, or when skin is a bit crispy. If you don't care about the skin, let it cook on one side until you see the fish turn opaque about halfway up, about 3-4 minutes. Flip with grill tongs, or tongs plus spatula. If the skin stays on the grill, no matter, just flip the fish to a spot just beside the skin. If you want to eat the skin, remove it with tongs at this point. Otherwise, let it burn on the grill and it will be easier to remove.

Cook about 2-3 minutes more and check to see if the fish is done. It should flake easily with a fork, but it doesn't have to be opaque all the way through unless you want it to be. If it isn't done, turn down the gas or move to the cooler part of the grill to finish cooking.

The dill actually stays with the fish better than you think it will, but some will fall off and burn.

SPAGHETTI AND MEAT SAUCE

Whole-wheat pasta
2 lb. of lean ground beef, cooked
1 diced onion, cook with beef
1 jar of organic no-sugar tomato sauce
1 garlic clove, minced
1/4 tsp. of sea salt
1 small can of tomato paste

Simmer all ingredients except pasta for 30 minutes.
Cook the whole-wheat pasta according to package directions and pour the sauce over the pasta.

SPAGHETTI SQUASH
AND MEAT SAUCE

Spaghetti squash is a good alternative to pasta, potatoes, or rice. The cooked squash flesh shreds into threads
like thin spaghetti or vermicelli, hence its name. On average, a spaghetti squash measures about 12 inches in length
and about 6 inches in diameter. The squash should be an
even, light yellow color and firm with no bruises. Store the
squash whole at room temperature for up to 3 weeks.
Spaghetti squash is available year-round with its peak season in fall.

Spaghetti squash has a very mild flavor, thus it is usually served with a sauce of some sort. It may also be

enjoyed simply with salt and a bit of butter. Cooking the squash is very simple.

Prick the spaghetti squash all over with a skewer so it will not burst while baking. Place whole squash in a shallow baking pan. Bake in preheated 375 F oven for 1 hour.

When cool enough to handle, cut spaghetti squash in half lengthwise with a serrated knife. Scoop the seeds and fibrous strings from the center of the cooked spaghetti squash. Gently scrape the tines of a kitchen fork around the edge of the spaghetti squash to shred the pulp into strands.

Serve with meat sauce recipe found earlier in this chapter.

SLOW COOKER
SPLIT PEA SOUP RECIPE

Total Time: 8 hours

1 (16 oz.) pkg. dried green split peas, rinsed
1 meaty hambone, 2 ham hocks, or 2 cups diced ham
3 carrots, peeled and sliced
1/2 c. chopped onion
2 ribs of celery plus leaves, chopped
1 or 2 cloves of garlic, minced
1 bay leaf
1/4 cup fresh parsley, chopped, or
2 teaspoons dried parsley flakes

1 tbsp. seasoned salt (or to taste)
1/2 tsp. fresh pepper
1 1/2 qts. hot water or chicken broth.

Layer ingredients in slow cooker in the order given;
pour in water. Do not stir ingredients. Cover and cook on
high 4 to 5 hours or on low 8 to 10 hours until peas are
very soft and ham falls off bone. Remove bones and bay
leaf. Mash peas to thicken soup, if desired. Serve garnished
with croutons. Freezes well. (Serves 8.)

STIR-FRY CHICKEN
AND VEGETABLES

1 lb. boneless chicken breast
2 tbsp. low sodium soy sauce
3 tbsp. coconut oil
2 minced garlic cloves
2 c. sliced mushrooms
2 c. broccoli
1 Tbsp. grated ginger
Bean sprouts

Cut chicken in cubes. Brown chicken in coconut oil
and soy sauce. Toss in broccoli and cook for 1 minute.
Add mushrooms and cook for 1 minute. Add ginger, bean
sprouts, and garlic--cook for additional 2 minutes. Put stir
fry over brown rice and serve.

STRAWBERRY VINEGARETTE DRESSING

1/2 c. olive oil
1/2 c. sliced strawberries
1 tsp. mustard
2 tbsp. red wine vinegar (balsamic is even
better, but carb counts vary, so be careful)
Salt and pepper to taste

Puree strawberries in a blender or food processor. Add vinegar, mustard, and seasonings. Blend, then add olive oil. Continue blending until creamy. Taste and adjust seasonings.

STUFFED CABBAGE

Prep Time: 20 minutes
Cook Time: 1 hour
Total Time: 1 hour, 20 minutes

This easy, healthy meal can be made either in the oven or a slow cooker (crockpot). I use a large, covered roasting pan, because the raw cabbage takes up so much space, but it shrinks a lot during cooking. The roots of this dish are Eastern European; there are variations of stuffed cabbage all over that region. This version has the same flavors and ingredients of stuffed cabbage, but is much easier! It can be made low fat by using very lean ground meat.

1 head cabbage

1 to 1 1/2 lbs. ground meat (turkey)

1/4 c. minced onion

1 tbsp. caraway seeds (optional, but highly recommended)

1 tsp. ground coriander (optional, but if you have any around, put it in)

1 tsp. garlic powder

1 can tomatoes (about 16 oz.— diced is nice, but whole is fine)

3 tbsp. lemon juice (can use vinegar, which is actually more traditional)

Honey

Salt, pepper

Cut the cabbage into chunks, about 3 inches on a side (you don't have to be exact). Separate into pieces, maybe 2 to 4 leaves thickness each. Put about half in the bottom of the roasting pan or crockpot.

Mix the meat, onion, and spices, including salt and pepper. Form into meatballs and nestle among the cabbage leaves. Put the rest of the leaves on top.

Put tomatoes and lemon juice or vinegar into blender (or into a pot and use a stick blender, or use a food processor). Pulse a few times. You want the tomatoes partially pureed, but still with a few chunks. You can fully puree half the can, if desired. You can do this in a pot on the stove and cook it down a bit if you want (it's actually probably best to do this in order to blend the flavors, but it's not crucial).

Add honey to the tomato mixture until you get a nice "sweet and sour" effect. Add a bit of salt and pepper, and another tablespoon of caraway seeds, if desired. Pour the mixture over the cabbage.

Bake in oven at 350 F for 1 hour. I like to cover it for the first 20 minutes to get the juices going, and then remove the cover. In a crockpot, cook for 6 to 8 hours on low or 2 to 3 on high. (Makes 4 servings, Per Serving: 15g. effective Carbohydrate; 9g. Fiber; 30 g. Protein.)

SWEET POTATO FRIES

Cut up sweet potato into size of fries. Coat the fries with olive oil and sprinkle with sea salt. Bake fries at 350 F for 15 to 20 minutes. Turn fries and cook additional 15 to 20 minutes. Cook longer for crispy fries.

THAI CHICKEN CURRY DISH

Prep Time: 20 minutes
Cook Time: 10 minutes
Total Time: 30 minutes

This is a simple skillet meal. You can use any curry you like. There are jars of Thai curry paste on the market of various types, or you can use a powdered mixture.

2 lb. skinless chicken breasts or thighs, cut
in bite-sized pieces
1 medium onion (optional, but I like it),
chopped
1 medium red bell pepper, chopped
12 oz. fresh or frozen green beans
1 or 2 cans coconut milk (can use light
or regular)
Thai curry spices, to taste (depends on heat)
Salt or seasoning salt to taste

Heat thin coating of coconut oil in pan.

Chop onion and add to pan.

Chop pepper and add to pan. Stir. Cook until onion is
getting soft, if it isn't already.

While that is cooking, chop the chicken.

Add the spices to the pan (including the salt). The
amount used will depend upon the spice. For example,
with Penzey's Sate' Seasoning, I use about 4 tsp, but for a
hot paste, I would use more like 2 tsp. It just depends
upon how spicy the blend is and how spicy you like your
food. Stir until you start to smell the spices.

Add the chicken to the pan. Stir until almost cooked
through.

Add the coconut milk. (Note: this makes a fairly soupy
curry. If you want it thicker, just add maybe 2/3 of the can
of coconut milk.) Bring the mixture to a boil, and simmer
for 3 to 5 minutes.

TOMATO AND CUCUMBER SALAD

4 medium tomatoes, each cut into 8 wedges
(about 3 cups)
2 medium cucumbers, thinly sliced
(about 5 cups)
1/2 cup finely chopped red onion
1/2 cup rice vinegar
1 tablespoon finely chopped fresh dill
1/2 teaspoon seasoned salt

In a large glass serving bowl, mix tomatoes, cucumbers and onion.

In a small bowl, mix all remaining ingredients until blended. Pour vinegar mixture over vegetables; toss to mix. Cover; refrigerate 1 hour to blend flavors. Toss again just before serving. Serve with slotted spoon.

For maximum cucumber crunch, choose firm, slender cucumbers with thin skins. Cucumber seeds become bitter with age. Slice older cucumbers in half lengthwise and run the tip of a spoon down the center to remove the seeds. Or try Hothouse cucumbers--these very long, slender cucumbers don't have many seeds but cost a bit more.

Rice vinegar is less acidic than cider, white or wine vinegar. Look for it near the other vinegars in the grocery store.

TURKEY BURGERS

2 lb. ground turkey meat
1 tsp. cumin
1/4 tsp. pepper
1/4 tsp. sea salt
1/4 tsp. white vinegar

Mix ingredients together to make patties. Grill or pan fry and serve with whole-grain bread.

TURKEY TACOS

2 lb. ground turkey meat
Taco shells
Lettuce
Tomato
Picante sauce

Brown turkey meat with sea salt and taco seasoning to taste. Warm taco shells, fill with ingredients and top off with picante sauce.

VEGETABLE SOUP

1 chopped onion
4 stalks of bok choy, chopped
1 bunch of celery, chopped
½ lb. of chopped carrots
½ tbsp. dried dill
2 tbsp. olive oil
1 tbsp. minced garlic
½ tsp. pepper
1 tbsp. sea salt
2 c. organic vegetable broth
10 c. of water

Combine all ingredients in crockpot. Cook on low for 4 hours. If you add chicken, you would use chicken broth instead of vegetable broth. Cook for 7 hours on low. The chicken can be cubed. You can freeze leftovers.

WATERMELON AND CUCUMBER SALAD

This salad is so refreshing, delicious, and easy to make. Because it is different, people like it at potlucks, and you can easily adjust it to make many portions or a few. Basically, it's half watermelon and half cucumber, with a sprinkling of mint and feta cheese. The saltiness of the cheese makes a surprisingly delicious contrast to the watermelon.

> 2 c. chopped watermelon
> 2 c. chopped cucumber
> 1/4 c. minced fresh mint
> 1/3 c. crumbled feta cheese

Mix watermelon, cucumber, and most of the mint and cheese together. Sprinkle remaining mint and cheese on top. Garnish with whole mint leaves if desired.

My Mission Statement

To help people, teach people and give them aid. To exhort and encourage, give practical service with a specific interest, expertise and knowledge in nutrition.

it's all about balance